Professional Practice in Governance and Public Organizations

"Professional Practice in Governance and Public Organizations" offers cutting-edge insights and practical guidance for professionals in the areas of economics, politics, public policy and public administration, and those working at international organizations. The series features concise and accessible books on the latest developments in governance, organizational and political strategies, institutional policies, policy instruments, public management, and finance. Leadership and digitalization issues are a core topic throughout the series. All volumes are written by practitioners, experts and leading authorities from think tanks, non-governmental organizations, and public and international organizations. While the books are explicitly intended for professionals in the above-mentioned fields, students of economics, political science, public policy and public administration will also benefit from these practical guides for their future careers.

Sapir Handelman

Solution-Focused Negotiation

From Family Disputes to Politics

 Springer

Sapir Handelman
Negoflict
Tel-Aviv, Israel

Minds of Peace
Tel-Aviv, Israel

Minds of Peace
St. Louis, USA

Conflict Studies Division, Liberal Arts
Department
Achva Academic College
Yinon, Israel

ISSN 2731-9776   ISSN 2731-9784   (electronic)
Professional Practice in Governance and Public Organizations
ISBN 978-3-031-52875-0   ISBN 978-3-031-52876-7   (eBook)
https://doi.org/10.1007/978-3-031-52876-7

© The Editor(s) (if applicable) and The Author(s), under exclusive license to Springer Nature Switzerland AG 2024

This work is subject to copyright. All rights are solely and exclusively licensed by the Publisher, whether the whole or part of the material is concerned, specifically the rights of reprinting, reuse of illustrations, recitation, broadcasting, reproduction on microfilms or in any other physical way, and transmission or information storage and retrieval, electronic adaptation, computer software, or by similar or dissimilar methodology now known or hereafter developed.

The use of general descriptive names, registered names, trademarks, service marks, etc. in this publication does not imply, even in the absence of a specific statement, that such names are exempt from the relevant protective laws and regulations and therefore free for general use.

The publisher, the authors, and the editors are safe to assume that the advice and information in this book are believed to be true and accurate at the date of publication. Neither the publisher nor the authors or the editors give a warranty, expressed or implied, with respect to the material contained herein or for any errors or omissions that may have been made. The publisher remains neutral with regard to jurisdictional claims in published maps and institutional affiliations.

This Springer imprint is published by the registered company Springer Nature Switzerland AG
The registered company address is: Gewerbestrasse 11, 6330 Cham, Switzerland

Paper in this product is recyclable.

*To my wife Yael
and
our daughters, Avia and Mia, who taught us the meaning of
unconditional love.*

Preface

Most people, in one way or another, are involved in conflicts in their daily, professional and political life. They tend to avoid dealing with their conflicts, even when the situation causes them a great deal of suffering. This book is written to introduce a powerful mechanism for conflict resolution—*Solution-Focused Negotiation*.

Solution-Focused Negotiation is an intensive peacemaking interaction. Disputing parties agree to take time-out from the routine of their daily life in order to negotiate solutions to their conflict. The interaction has rules, structure and a timeframe. *Solution-Focused Negotiation* is a social instrument for reaching practical and enforceable solutions to conflicts in a limited time frame.

I have led, directly and indirectly, dozens of face-to-face and online Solution-Focused Negotiations. My colleagues, students and I have helped many people to successfully cope with their conflicts. The cases include tensions, frictions and struggles in almost all dimensions of our social life, from family disputes to politics. My goal is to share my knowledge, experience and expertise with scholars, practitioners and ordinary people.

Sigmund Freud dreamed of making psychotherapy accessible to everyone. Our experience shows that online communication can bring the art of *Solution-Focused Negotiation* to almost every adult in the world. The use of technology can turn "ordinary people" into "super mediators". This is the beginning of a social revolution—'The Mediating Revolution'.

Tel-Aviv, Israel
July 2023

Sapir Handelman

Acknowledgments I would like to thank my colleagues and friends who helped me organize and lead *Solution-Focused Negotiations* in various settings, forms and formats: Nir Caftori—my *Negoflict* partner; Ofer Lidror and Miki Dotan—my *Minds of Peace* partners in Israel; Daniel Mahgerefteh, Ron Fredman and Hannan Lis—my *Minds of Peace* partners in the US; and Tzili Charney, founder of the Charney Resolution Center.

Contents

1	**Introduction**	1
2	**Solution-Focused Negotiation**	5
	Conflict and Negotiation	6
	Resolvable and Irresolvable Conflicts	8
	Micro-conflicts—Macro-solutions	12
	The Building Blocks	13
	Four Variables	19
	Notes	20
	References	20
3	**The Mediator's Trap**	21
	Intractable Conflict—An Unending Story	22
	Barriers and Game Changers	24
	Strategic and Tactical Barriers	26
	The Trap of a Problem-Solving Mediator—Competition and Cooperation	29
	The Trap of a Power Mediator: Who is the "Real" Manipulator?	32
	'Islands of Agreement'—Points of Agreement Within Disagreements	34
	Negotiators Know the Solutions at the Beginning of the Process	35
	The Game Changer	36
	The First Agreement and the Strategic Mistake	37
	The Second Agreement and the Limits of Shuttle Negotiation	40

Concluding Remarks	42
Notes	43
References	44

4 Three Types of Negotiation — 45

Negotiating with the Devil — 45
Bargaining, Problem-Solving and Consensus-Building — 49
The Historical Debate—Realism, Pluralism and Contractualism — 50
Realism—Negotiation as Bargaining — 50
   The Limits of Realism — 52
Pluralism—Negotiation as Problem-Solving — 53
   The First Experiment—Manipulation, Negotiation and Problem-Solving — 55
   Negotiation as Problem-Solving—The Limitations — 56
Contractualism—Negotiation as Consensus-Building — 59
   Conflict in Northern Ireland — 59
   The Need for a Different Approach — 61
   Contractualism—A Third Paradigm in Peace and Conflict Studies — 61
   Negotiating with the Devil—The All-Party Talks — 63
   The All-Party Talks—A Consensus-Building Device — 64
   Dead-Line—Last-Ditch Effort — 66
   The Final Episode — 67
Concluding Remarks — 68
Notes — 70
References — 72

5 Transformation — 75

Negotiating Cooperative — 76
Motivation—A Strong Desire to Solve the Conflict by Peaceful Means — 78
   Ripe Moment for Negotiation — 79
   Different Perspectives, Creating Value and Back-Door Mediation — 80
Rules—Commitment to Constructive Rules of Negotiation — 83
   Two General Ground Rules — 84
   Two Interactive Systems of Thinking and Operation — 84
   First Rule—Do Not Demean One Another and Do Show Respect — 85
   Second Rule—Avoid Historical Debate about the Origin of the Conflict and Past Evils — 87
   Historical Justice Versus Practical Justice — 89

Negotiating Platform	90
Human Limitations and Support Systems	91
Visionary Mediator	94
Concluding Remarks	96
Notes	97
References	97

6 Practicality — 99
Binary Trap — 99
Resolvable and Irresolvable Conflicts — 102
Conflicts of Interests — 105
Leaders Who Did Not Know How to Negotiate — 106
Cognitive Biases and the Binary Trap — 109
Concluding Remarks — 112
Notes — 116
References — 116

7 Discovery — 117
Three Types of Game Changers — 117
Negotiation as a Discovery Procedure — 119
Ideal Mediators and Key Game Changers — 120
Three Forms of Negotiation and Key Game Changers — 121
Positional Bargaining—Islands of Agreement — 125
Problem-Solving Cooperative—Changing Concepts — 129
  'Working Trust' and 'Basic Trust'—Political Dispute — 129
  'Working Trust' and 'Basic Trust'—Family Dispute — 132
  'Working Trust' as a Key Game Changer — 134
Consensus-Building—Supportive Environment — 135
Concluding Remarks — 138
Notes — 140
References — 140

In Conclusion — 143

References — 145

Index — 149

1

Introduction

I was sitting in a coffee shop at the center of Tel-Aviv. The atmosphere in the streets was unpleasant, to say the least. It was during the war between Hamas and Israel, which started on October 7, 2023. I was trying to finish the last chapter of this book. It was an awful time. The ongoing news from the war was depressing. Once in a while we heard a siren—an alert for a rocket or missile attack—and had to run down to the bomb shelter.

The situation in my family was also tense. Schools did not operate as usual. My young daughters were at home most of the time. They demanded—and, of course, deserved—my attention, the attention of their dad. Every free moment was precious and I had to use my time effectively and efficiently.

I was doing my best to concentrate on writing the book in the coffee shop. Suddenly, a young guy approached me. "Do you remember me?" he asked. I did not recognize the guy. "No", I replied. "You helped me to negotiate my salary", the guy said. "Ok", I mumbled, "And, how did it go?" The guy smiled, "I followed your advice and I got a significant increase in salary". "I am very happy for you", I said. "And, now I need to continue working".

The guy acted like he did not hear my polite request to be left alone. He came to sit next to me, "I have another problem with negotiation. I want to ask for your advice and recommendations". I realized that this is a hopeless situation for me. The guy is not going to give up. And, I know my weaknesses. Convincing others to not cross my personal boundaries is not easy for me, especially when they need help.

At first sight, it might seem strange that I am writing a book about Solution-Focused Negotiation. I consider myself to be a lousy negotiator when it comes to my private concerns. My family, friends and students know that it is not difficult to take advantage of my emotional weaknesses. I tend to be too soft and surrender too easily, especially about matters that concern my personal interests. However, I know, quite well, how to help disputing parties reach agreements.

I am very sensitive to human suffering and misery. I love helping people. I have led—directly and indirectly—different conflict resolution settings, procedures and processes. I have aided many people from different walks of life cope with their personal, professional and political struggles. My colleagues and I have developed a powerful tool to cope with conflicts—Solution-Focused Negotiation.

Two seminal books offer different approaches to negotiation. The first is *Getting to Yes*, written by Harvard negotiation scholars, Fisher, Ury and Patton. The second is *Never Split the Difference*, written by a former FBI hostage negotiator, Chris Voss.

Getting to Yes suggests negotiation strategies that appeal to the rational mind of adversaries. In contrast, *Never Split the Difference* offers methods that appeal to the emotional mind of antagonists. Solution-Focused Negotiation suggests treating these competitive approaches as complementary. Opposing parties entrenched in a bitter conflict need a method that approaches the situation from various sides, directions and dimensions.

Solution-Focused Negotiation is an intensive conflict resolution process. Adversaries take time-out from their daily routine to negotiate practical and enforceable solutions to their conflict. The initiative has rules, structure and a timetable. This book demonstrates that almost everyone can mediate conflicts and improve their negotiation skills.

The book is written to share the knowledge that my colleagues and I accumulated by leading various online and face-to-face events of Solution-Focused Negotiation. It has two parts. The first part—Chaps. 2–4—is an introduction to the study and practice of negotiation and mediation. It clarifies basic concepts in the art of negotiation, such as resolvable and irresolvable conflicts, strategic and tactical barriers, and different kinds of negotiation. This first part sketches the landscape of negotiation and describes the advantages and limitations of this conflict resolution tool.

The second part—Chaps. 5–7—describes the structure, framework and operation of Solution-Focused Negotiation. It demonstrates how to use this powerful instrument for the benefit of the negotiators.

This book is a part of a lifetime project. The project is to impart knowledge and skills to cope with conflicts to each one of us. Solution-Focused Negotiation is one of the main instruments to reach this goal. My colleagues and I are developing the Negoflict system, a digital platform for Solution-Focused Negotiation that will serve each one of us as negotiator and mediator. Various examples in this book demonstrate the potential of Negoflict to create a revolution in human relations.

I hope you will enjoy the book.

2

Solution-Focused Negotiation
From Family Disputes to Politics

Solution-Focused Negotiation is a powerful conflict resolution tool. It can be applied in almost all dimensions of social life, from family relations to international politics. The initiative invites disputing parties to negotiate practical solutions to conflicts. The negotiation is conducted in a framework of rules, structure and timeline.

History shows that a Solution-Focused Negotiation can be a powerful tool to reach agreement between adversaries. An example is the Atlantic City Conference of 1929 which is considered to be the event that turned the American Mafia into a multi-ethnic organized crime syndicate. Representatives of crime families, which had been competing with each other, came to a 3-day conference to negotiate principles for cooperation and settling internal conflicts by 'peaceful' means. As we can see even today, the results of this meeting benefited rival criminal gangs by being the first step toward the creation of a proto-confederation of multi-criminal entities.

Another classic example is the Camp David Accords of 1978. During 13 days of intensive negotiations, Jimmy Carter, the President of the US, succeeded in brokering a peace agreement between the Israeli Prime Minister, Menachem Begin, and the Egyptian President, Anwar Sadat. Since then, Egypt and Israel—former entrenched enemies—have engaged in a cold peace. It was a turning point in the history of the Middle East, in general, and the Arab–Israeli conflict, in particular.

There have also been unsuccessful cases of Solution-Focused Negotiation. About 22 years after the first Camp David Accords, the President of the US, Bill Clinton, tried to recreate the success of President Carter. President Clinton invited the Israeli Prime Minister, Ehud Barak, and the Palestinian leader, Yasser Arafat, for 14 days of Solution-Focused Negotiation at Camp David. Unfortunately, the summit failed. It ended without an agreement.

The results of the 2000 Camp David Summit's failure to reach a negotiated solution to the Israeli-Palestinian conflict were a disaster. This failure was followed by another cycle of violence between Israelis and Palestinians (the Second Intifada) and a paradigm shift. The conflict-management paradigm—constructing strategies and tactics to reduce the level of violence in a tragic situation of irresolvable conflict—became the dominant paradigm among Israeli leaders and scholars. The Israeli-Palestinian struggle remained one of the most entrenched conflicts in the world.

Why do some negotiating initiatives succeed, while others fail? What is the most effective and efficient structure, construction and operation of Solution-Focused Negotiation? How can we bring this powerful conflict resolution instrument into our daily lives?

This chapter serves as an introduction to the book as a whole. It introduces the concept of Solution-Focused Negotiation as a conflict resolution tool and a relationship-building instrument. It briefly describes the operative modes of this peacemaking instrument, demonstrates its various applications and sketches the landscape of its effectiveness.

Let us begin our journey with the clarification of key concepts in negotiation and conflict studies. The purpose is to create a language and terminology for the study and operation of Solution-Focused Negotiation.

Conflict and Negotiation

Conflict, according to this book, is a problem with different demands for its resolution. Severe and entrenched conflicts are, often enough, the result of agreement and not necessarily disagreement. A classic example is a fight over the possession of the family house between a married couple in a divorce proceeding. Both the husband and the wife love their family home. They agree that the house is valuable, comfortable and in the perfect location. Each of them demands it for himself or herself. Both Israelis and Palestinians believe that Jerusalem is valuable, precious and holy. They are fighting for it.

Negotiation is a process by which opposing parties attempt to reach agreements that can settle their conflict by peaceful means. Solution-Focused Negotiation is an intensive version of negotiating interaction. It is a social instrument for reaching practical and enforceable solutions to conflicts in a limited timeframe.

Solution-Focused Negotiation can be an efficient and effective instrument for reaching agreement. This social tool can have a major impact on the relationship between the parties. The influence of the negotiating process and its outcomes on social relationships can be a very important aspect of the interaction. It is especially significant in situations, such as family disputes, where future contact between the parties—whether they desire it or not—is inevitable.

The impact of Solution-Focused Negotiation on social relationships can lead to a conflict of interests. On the one hand, each party wishes to reach the best deal for himself or herself (competitive motivation). On the other hand, the disputing parties still have an interest to maintain good relationship, especially in situations where future contact is unavoidable (cooperative motivation).

The competitive motivation—maximizing the deal—can have a bad influence on the relationship between the parties and their relationships with their social environments. However, a cooperative and less competitive attitude of, at least, one party—who tries to maintain good relationships and avoid a full-scale war—can motivate this negotiator to compromise too easily and accept a bad deal. A bad deal can damage the well-being of the "moderate" negotiator with a disastrous influence on the future relationship with the other side.

This conflict of interests—competition (maximizing the deal) versus cooperation (maximizing the relationship) —is often called *the negotiator's dilemma*.[1] Negotiators face a dilemma in choosing their attitude, behavior and actions. Each negotiator has to decide whether to pursue a competitive strategy, which endangers the relationship between the parties, or a cooperative strategy, that might lead to terrible outcomes for his or her well-being.

A married couple can divorce each other but they cannot divorce their children. A bitter fight around the negotiating table over the appropriate division of their property (for selfish reasons) can destroy their relationship. This competitive process and its side effects can have a very bad influence on the well-being of the children. However, a negotiating party who compromises too easily—in order to avoid war, maintain a good relationship and protect the children—can also pay a heavy price. This negotiator can end up with a very bad financial deal which can damage his or her well-being. In the long run, such a compromising strategy can have a negative impact on the relationship with the former spouse and produce bad outcomes for the children.

"Winning" the negotiation can be a Pyrrhic victory, "a victory that comes at a great cost, perhaps making the ordeal to win not worth it".[2] However, "losing" the negotiation for the sake of a greater value and cause (such as the benefit of the children) can lead to financial bankruptcy. An effective Solution-Focused Negotiation navigates the parties to overcome the negotiator's dilemma (the clash between competitive and cooperative motivations).

This book suggests looking at Solution-Focused Negotiation as a deal-making instrument and a relationship-building device. The most successful cases of Solution-Focused Negotiation helped the parties reach a settlement of mutual benefit and opened possibilities for a good relationship and cooperation. An ideal interaction balances the two aspects of the initiative (competition and cooperation). The question is: How to approach this ideal?

Let us sketch the landscape of effective negotiating interaction in order to create a basis and a framework to deal with this question.

Resolvable and Irresolvable Conflicts

Conflict, according to this book, is a problem with different demands for its resolution. A classic example is a beautiful young woman that two young men, Rudolf Valentino and Don Juan, wish to marry. Both of them agree that she could be the perfect wife. Each one of them demands the young woman for himself.

To define the playground of a negotiating interaction, it is important to distinguish between resolvable and irresolvable conflicts. In this book, I define a resolvable conflict as a negotiable struggle—a conflict that, in principle, can be resolved through negotiation. In contrast, an irresolvable conflict is a non-negotiable struggle—a conflict that, in principle, it is impossible to resolve by negotiation.

Rudolf Valentino and Don Juan, who want to marry the same young woman, cannot negotiate their feelings. For example, it is impossible to negotiate a proposal where Don Juan will love the lady in the first half of the week and Rudolf Valentino—his competitor—will care for her only during the second half of the week. However, in principle, they can negotiate a practical and enforceable settlement that addresses their interests to impress the lady. For example, they can negotiate an arrangement that allows Don Juan to spend time and impress the young woman from Sunday to Tuesday, and Rudolf Valentino will have his chance to win her heart from Wednesday to Friday. Hopefully, on Saturday, the lady will make a decision. She can choose one of them as her future husband or walk away from any romantic involvement with these "great lovers".

Conflicts that belong to the mental sphere, such as viewpoints, beliefs and emotions, are not negotiable. It is impossible to measure and exchange feelings, beliefs and viewpoints. And, it is impossible to find a practical and enforceable solutions to these kinds of conflicts. As far as I know, we do not have any devices that can read, measure and monitor our thoughts and feelings. Therefore, according to our definition, such conflicts are irresolvable. In contrast, conflicts that belong to the physical sphere—conflicts that focus on issues that can be measured and calculated, such as interests, options and resources—are negotiable. According to our definition, these conflicts are resolvable.

Unfortunately, it is quite common for human beings to try to negotiate the impossible, to "negotiate" viewpoints, beliefs and emotions. These interactions can very quickly deteriorate into frustrated debates and unproductive blame games. This phenomenon appears in our daily life when the talks do not have rules, structure and guidance. In one of our first case studies, a mother and her teenage daughter, who agreed to accept our help, were caught in this trap.

A friend of mine and I were sitting in a coffee shop. We discussed the idea of building a digital platform for Solution-Focused Negotiation. A mother and her two daughters were dining at the table next to us. I used my Israeli chutzpah to approach them and tell them about our project. I asked them if they have a conflict that they would agree to try to settle by using online Text Messenger. I offered my help as a mediator. I explained that it would be a very good experience for them and a valuable experiment for us.

The mother told us about a bitter conflict that she has with her younger daughter. The topic was: the appropriate time that the young lady should return home after hanging out with friends. Each of their attempts to discuss the issue turned into a frustrated debate on a non-negotiable question: Is this teenage girl mature enough to take responsibility for her lifestyle or not?

The young lady claimed that she is mature enough to take care of herself and decide upon the appropriate time to come back home. The mother claimed that her daughter is still young and not fully aware of all the dangers outside at night. Each of their attempts to discuss the issue ended with a fight. They were locked in a frustrated positional debate and did not listen to one another. This unproductive debate created a bad atmosphere at home. We engaged them in online Solution-Focused Negotiation. I led the talks. We named the conflict: "Curfew Time".

The starting point was their main problem: "What is the appropriate time the young lady should return home from going out with her friends?" This time the talks focused on different solutions to the problem and the logic and motivations behind them. The online communication and the rules of the game enabled them to listen to one another. They began to understand the needs and fears of each other and examine practical arrangements that can solve their problem. The talks converged to a negotiable pragmatic question: "What is the appropriate balance between the young lady's need to hang out late with her friends and her mother's fear for her safety and well-being?".

The structured negotiation kept them from sliding to the old familiar frustrated debate on a non-negotiable problem (a clash between beliefs and viewpoints): the daughter's degree of maturity. Surprisingly, it turned out that safety was a common concern. We were astonished to find out that the young lady, usually, wishes to return home quite early. She comes home late because she does not have anyone to escort her. Her friends like to hang out late.

This discovery was a game changer. It enabled to turn the mother and her daughter into a problem-solving team. They quite easily reached an agreement on the appropriate time for the daughter to return home and found an arrangement to guarantee her safety. They agreed that once a week the daughter will hang out with her friends until 1:30 am. She will come home with a taxi. Her mother will order the cab and finance it.

Resolvable conflict centers around a negotiable problem—a problem that, in principle, can be resolved through negotiation. The inspiration for this criterion is the Falsification Principle of the great philosopher of science, Sir Karl Popper. This principle offers a general criterion to distinguish between science and non-science. It suggests that a theory is scientific only if it is possible, in principle, to test and refute it.

A resolvable conflict does not mean that we will succeed in resolving it around the negotiation table. Success is not guaranteed. It only means that, in principle, it is possible to reach a negotiated solution to the struggle by peaceful means.

In principle, Israelis and Palestinians can negotiate practical solutions to a permanent status and management of the holy places in Jerusalem. They can search for negotiated solutions that satisfy religious sentiments of different believers and enable them to worship the Divine respectfully, peacefully and safely. Moreover, different arrangements have been suggested by different scholars and practitioners. Unfortunately, Israeli and Palestinian leaderships did not succeed to reach a permanent negotiated arrangement that would solve this sensitive problem.

In cases such as the Israeli-Palestinian conflict, the first challenge is to bring the opposing leaders to the negotiating table. The next challenge is to build the conditions for successful interaction. The 2000 Camp David Summit succeeded in engaging Israeli and Palestinian leaders in a Solution-Focused Negotiation to their struggle. But it failed to bring peace, tranquility and stability to the region. The discussion about the permanent status of the holy places in Jerusalem was one of the main reasons for this tragic failure.

The famous political scientist Samuel Huntington argued that a main source of modern conflicts is the Clash of Civilizations. Cultural and religious confrontations are the motivating vehicle of major contemporary conflicts. The conflict over the holy places in Jerusalem can be presented, examined and analyzed in terms of the Clash of Civilizations theory. It can be viewed as a manifestation of ongoing confrontations between cultural and religious global forces.

Approaching a conflict from a Clash of Civilizations perspective is likely to lead any negotiation to a dead-end. It presents the conflict in non-negotiable terms. The negotiations in the 2000 Camp David Summit seem to have fallen into this trap.

At this summit, a frustrated theological and religious debate replaced a pragmatic and practical negotiation. Each negotiating party, Israeli and Palestinian, brought theological arguments to demonstrate the holiness of the sites to its religion. They were involved in unproductive competitive discussion. Each side tried to bring "religious proofs" that it has the first right over Jerusalem. Ironically, the negotiating team, at least from the Israeli side of the table, did not include theology experts and religious leaders.[3]

The negotiation turned into a debate between different viewpoints. It did not help the "negotiators" to reach their goal: finding the "optimal" formula to divide the holy city of Jerusalem between Israelis and Palestinians. As far as I know, they did not consider approaching the conflict from fresh and innovative perspectives. For example, they did not consider the idea that the area belongs to everybody and should not be divided. It could be monitored jointly by Israelis and Palestinians or, perhaps, it could be managed by a religious council with representatives of the three main monotheistic religions—Islam, Christianity and Judaism.

It is common knowledge that science progresses by approaching the same old problems from fresh perspectives. The same applies to problems in human relationships. Approaching a conflict from a pragmatic viewpoint can change the whole negotiating game. An efficient Solution-Focused Negotiation setting is designed to get the parties to approach their conflict from a point of view that is different from the one they are used to.

Indeed, it is possible to look at the Israeli-Palestinian conflict as a communal struggle rather than identifying it as part of a global clash between different civilizations. A pragmatic approach suggests examining the conflict as a struggle between two identity groups who are destined to live side by side, whether they are happy about it or not. The practical challenge is to find the optimal arrangement to peacefully share the land.

Israelis and Palestinians, in principle, can negotiate an appropriate arrangement that takes into account their interests and needs. For example, "What is the optimal social order that enables believers of different religions to peacefully warship the Devine in Jerusalem?" is a negotiable question.

Indeed, Israeli and Palestinian delegations of ordinary citizens in the various rounds of the *Minds of Peace Experiment*[4]—a small-scale Israeli-Palestinian Public Negotiating Congress that my colleagues and I have led in various formats, forms and locations—repeatedly succeeded in reaching negotiated solutions to these kinds of questions. The delegations in each round included people from the entire political spectrum. Our next problem is to bring these astonishing results to the operating political arena. It is not easy.

What are the main elements of an effective Solution-Focused Negotiation? How do we build a successful negotiating interaction? How do we build a negotiating interaction that has the greatest potential to create a positive change in the relationship between the parties?

To cope with these important questions, we need a theory and a model.

Micro-conflicts—Macro-solutions

Micro-conflicts center around one principle main issue, for example: the location of the family house, the size of the wedding and a decent salary for workers. Micro-conflicts do not threaten to destroy the world order—such as the Second World War or the Cuban Missile Crisis. But they still can create a great deal of misery and suffering, sometimes on a daily basis.

Micro-conflicts emerge in almost all dimensions of our social life, from family relations to politics. Married couples regularly argue about the appropriate division of the household chores, and professional politicians constantly fight over the most suitable place for their weekly meetings. Problematic communication is a major symptom of micro-conflicts.

One of the main goals of this book is to enable ordinary people to habitually and successfully use conflict resolution tools. Our instrument to achieve this goal is a Solution-Focused Negotiation. We constructed a simple model to cope with micro-conflicts.

Table 2.1 Solution-focused negotiation as a good story

A good story	Solution-focused negotiation
Tittle	Tittle
Prologue	The problem
Introduction	Rules and framework
Beginning	Opening positions
The main plot	Negotiation
Twist in the plot	Key game changer
Summary	Agreements

Our model, which is described in Table 2.1, is designed to construct Solution-Focused Negotiation like a work of art, a short story. It has a beginning, development, twist in the main plot and, often enough, an unexpected end. Of course, this description is an idealistic simplification of reality. The following section presents a Solution-Focused Negotiation model that can help us approach the ideal.

Research shows that people who succeed in changing a bad habit (such as smoking) experience a major change in their behavior and lifestyle.[5] My students who participated in online Solution-Focused Negotiation reported that the initiative helped them improve their relationship and communication with their social environment.

Is it a long-lasting change or only a temporary one? How do we use Solution-Focused Negotiation as a deal-making tool and relationship-building instrument? Can this activity help ordinary people customarily have a conflict resolution attitude?

Let us start by presenting the building blocks of our model of a Solution-Focused Negotiation.

The Building Blocks

Solution-Focused Negotiation rests on three pillars:

Transformation—turning opposing parties into a negotiating cooperative.

Practicality—focusing on practical solutions to a negotiable problem.

Discovery—discovering key game changers.

In the second part of the book, Chaps. 5–7, I explain in detail and demonstrate the potential contribution of each one of these elements to the success of negotiation. This book shows that an effective combination of these three elements has the greatest potential to build, maintain and successfully conclude a Solution-Focused Negotiation. Let me briefly introduce these three building blocks.

1. *Transformation—turning opposing parties into a negotiating cooperative*

Four elements are necessary to turn opposing parties into a negotiating cooperative:

1. **Motivation**—a strong desire to resolve the conflict by peaceful means.
2. **Rules**—agreement on principles of constructive dialogue, such as: not to demean one another.
3. **Platform**—a negotiating platform that provides channels for productive talks, such as direct and indirect means of communication.
4. **Leadership**—a visionary mediator is required, especially in situations of difficult and entrenched conflicts, to build the negotiating cooperative and operate it for the benefit of the negotiators.

The transformation of the opposing parties into a negotiating cooperative creates commitment to the process. Commitment is a necessary condition for effective negotiation, especially in difficult situations of conflict. In these circumstances, the interaction is in constant danger of collapsing. Commitment is necessary for keeping the process alive, helping the parties overcome difficult moments and motivating them to conclude agreements. Moreover, commitment to the process explains why negotiators behave differently around the negotiating table than one would expect at the beginning of the process. Our experience and experiments show clearly that negotiators, often enough, reach agreements that contradict their initial positions and declarations.

Menachem Begin, the Israeli right-wing hardline Prime Minister, brought historic peace between Israel and Egypt, while his "leftist" predecessor, Golda Meir, was in tenure during the traumatic October War of 1973 (the Yom Kippur War). Begin participated in a Solution-Focused Negotiation at Camp David in 1978. He negotiated peace with the President of Egypt, Anwar Sadat, under the mediation of the US President, Jimmy Carter. One of the main products of the summit was the agreement—"A Framework for Peace in the Middle East".

In the next chapter, I show that this agreement contradicts the traditional position of Begin and his right-wing ideology. Our experience shows that such a dramatic and drastic shift can happen to each one of us who participate in Solution-Focused Negotiation. Commitment of negotiators to the process can balance their commitment to their initial viewpoint, faith and ideology. It enables negotiators to examine critically their beliefs and reconsider (negotiate with themselves) their initial demands.

The transformation of opposing parties into a negotiating cooperative still does not guarantee success. The topic of the negotiation (the problem) is critical for the success of the interaction. Negotiating a non-negotiable problem is likely to lead the process to a dead-end. The next pillar of Solution-Focused Negotiation—Practicality—is designed to cope with this issue.

2. *Practicality—Focusing on Practical Solutions to a Negotiable Problem*

The topic of the negotiation—the problem—needs to be carefully chosen and presented. Trying to negotiate the impossible—a non-negotiable problem—can lead to destructive communication. The negotiating parties can waste time and effort in unproductive debate that can quite easily deteriorate into a blame game with slanders and intimidations. This destructive pattern of communication tends to repeat itself, even without the intent of the parties.

The transformation phase—turning the opposing parties into a negotiating cooperative—is a very important step in the road to reach a settlement. The parties commit to the rules, structure and procedure of the negotiating game. However, commitment to constructive form of dialogue is not enough to ensure productive negotiation. It is critical for the negotiating parties—whether they are family members, business partners or professional politicians—to focus on a resolvable (negotiable) problem.

It is almost impossible to negotiate feelings, beliefs and viewpoints. However, it is possible and desirable to negotiate practical options, resources and interests. A married couple cannot negotiate their amounts of feelings, concerns and attachment to their children. Questions about beliefs, feelings and viewpoints—such as, who cares more for the children—are non-negotiable matters. Focusing on a non-negotiable problem is a proven recipe for the collapse of the negotiation. It happened at the 2000 Camp David Summit—a Solution-Focused Negotiation between experienced political leaders—and it constantly happens to ordinary people who are trying to negotiate the terms of their divorce.

In situations of conflict, there are pragmatic questions that need to be addressed: How to guarantee that believers of the three monotheistic religions—Christianity, Islam and Judaism—will be able to peacefully, respectfully and safely express their religious feelings in the Old City of Jerusalem?

How to construct a decent democracy that protects the rights of the Catholic minority in Northern Ireland? What is the optimal divorce arrangement that can create balance between the interests, needs and fears of the separating spouses?

Pragmatic questions address genuine problems that can be very difficult to solve. Coping with these important questions, often enough, requires a lot of intellectual and mental effort. It seems to be much "easier" to blame the other side for creating the problems rather than to search for practical and creative solutions that can satisfy both sides. Unfortunately, in many cases the negotiating parties choose the "easy" way.

It is quite common for "negotiating" parties to enter into historical debate about the source of the conflict and past evils: "Who created the problem?", "Who did what to whom?" and "Who was right and who was wrong all the way?". This kind of historical discussion can quite easily turn the negotiation into a competitive blame game and deteriorate the relationship between the parties. If such historical debates occur during negotiation, I suggest labeling them "the history trap".

In difficult situations of conflict, each side tends to develop its own version of the story of the conflict. Israelis and Palestinians hold different narratives of their struggle; Catholics and Protestants in Northern Ireland present different perspectives of the origins of their struggle; husbands and wives tell different stories about the sources and causes of their constant fights.

In most cases, these narratives have true and false elements. They are mostly subjective constructions of reality. Nevertheless, each side believes, or at least presents, its own version of the history of the conflict as the ultimate truth ("God's words"). Historical debate upon the origins of the conflict in negotiation is likely to lead the interaction to a frustrated clash between viewpoints and beliefs. Since it is impossible to negotiate viewpoints and beliefs, the "negotiation" is likely to reach a dead-end.

The different narratives, often enough, contradict each other. They work like a mirror image. Elements of one narrative could be the ultimate truth for one side and a complete fake for the other. The US President Bill Clinton learned this lesson first hand.

In 1995, President Clinton visited London (England), Dublin (Republic of Ireland) and Belfast (Northern Ireland). The purpose was to create a momentum for an effective peace process in one of the most entrenched conflicts in the world—the 'troubles' in Northern Ireland. During the visit, the President met with leaders of the opposing camps—Catholics and Protestants—separately. Each leader had twenty minutes to present his view of the conflict to the President.

Senator George Mitchell—the independent chairman of the peace talks—describes this amazing scene in his memoir. Each side presented an integrated, fascinating and persuasive story. Each story seemed to be built like a work of art. However, those well-told stories of the same conflict were completely different and even contradicted each other.[6]

Neighboring communities, such as Catholics and Protestants in Northern Ireland and Israelis and Palestinians in the Middle East—whether they like it or not—are destined to live side by side. Married couples usually are not required to stay together. The option of getting a divorce usually exists. Nevertheless, often enough, unhappy married couples prefer staying together and continue causing misery to each other. Part of the problem is ongoing futile attempts to negotiate the impossible—negotiating unsolvable (non-negotiable) problems.

Our experience shows that it is quite common for a married couple to complain about detachment, cold relationship and lack of intimacy. In one of our cases, a husband demanded that his wife will love him more. It is impossible to negotiate the desired quantity of love between couples and it is impossible to reach an enforceable agreement that guarantees commitment to a certain amount of affection.

Focusing on resolvable problems—such as, what has to be done to keep the marriage alive, to maintain a good atmosphere at home and to bring intimacy back to their relationship—can creates miracles. Indeed, it is no coincidence that one of the main keys to the success of Brief Solution-Focused Therapy—which is significantly similar to Solution-Focused Negotiation—is labeled 'the miracle question'.

Presenting a negotiable question enabled the couple to take time-out from their old patterns of fighting and explore creative solutions to their problem. For example, they can decide to go to see a movie together once a week, have a romantic dinner once a month and travel abroad together twice a year.

We can assume that the married couple in our case agreed to participate in Solution-Focused Negotiation in order to improve their relationship. They committed to the framework—rules, structure and timetable—in order to examine possibilities for change. Their motivation to solve the conflict and their commitment to the process enabled them to form a negotiation cooperative (Transformation). The next challenge is to effectively operate the cooperative and keep the process alive. One of the main keys to success is the topic of the negotiation—the negotiated problem. The talks should focus on a resolvable problem—a problem that, in principle, can be solved via a negotiating process.

Unfortunately, some couples prefer to continue fighting over viewpoints—such as, 'who is right and who is wrong'—rather than negotiating practical measures to improve their marriage. Solution-Focused Negotiation—an intensive short-term interaction—needs to be pragmatic to overcome this trap. The key is to focus on practical solutions to a resolvable (negotiable) problem. Otherwise, the interaction is in danger of collapsing.

3. *Discovery—Detecting Key Game Changers*

Transformation and practicality are necessary elements for effective Solution-Focused Negotiation. Transformation turns opposing parties into a negotiation cooperative whose members are committed to resolve the conflict by peaceful means. Practicality intends to guarantee pragmatic discussion on a resolvable problem.

The combination of transformation and practicality—commitment of opposing parties to a pragmatic search for solutions to their conflict—is a necessary step on the road to resolve conflicts. But it is not a sufficient one. The establishment of a committed and pragmatic negotiation cooperative still does not guarantee success.

Often enough, negotiating partners—who are fully committed to the process—do not know how to progress toward resolution of the conflict. They face barriers to successfully conclude a Solution-Focused Negotiation. They do not have the knowledge to overcome these obstacles. They need a powerful element that enables them to examine the conflict from a fresh—imagined or unimagined—perspective. They need a game changer.

The game changer can be a piece of information, an innovative idea or even a manipulative attitude. The game changer illuminates the conflict with a different and unexpected light. This short story can demonstrate the game changer effect.

Two young guys fought over the only free seat on a bus. Neither of them showed any signs of giving up. The sophisticated driver approached them and asked a simple question: "Why do you need to sit?".

One of the guys claimed he needs to sit down because of his back problems. The other explained that sitting in this specific seat is a precious opportunity to get close to the beautiful lady that sits next to it. Unexpectedly, the young lady stood up, introduced herself and invited the guy to chat with her in the back of the bus. That conflict was resolved.

Albert Einstein changed the conventional and intuitive wisdom that mass (the quantity of material) is always fixed. His revolutionary perception was a game changer. It enabled scientists to examine the same old problems from a fresh perspective. The result was a major change in the science of physics.

Game changers in a Solution-Focused Negotiation can have similar effects on the way disputing parties perceive their conflict. For example, in property disputes, especially in divorce cases, it is quite common for the parties to believe that the pie—the size of the property in dispute—is fixed. This is a proven recipe for a zero-sum game.

Ironically, most of the time, this is not true. The pie—the property in dispute—is not fixed. The pie can shrink—for example, by going to court and paying expensive legal fees—and it can be enlarged—for example, the dispute is not only about the division of property, it is also about the mental and physical well-being of the children.

Solution-Focused Negotiation is a discovery procedure. It is the art of finding key game changers that can help disputing parties overcome deadlocks. Discovering constructive game changers sometimes seems to be a wizard's task. It requires constructive listening, imagination, creativity, knowledge and the ability to maneuver between different methods of negotiation—bargaining, problem-solving and consensus-building.

Game changers enable mediators and negotiators to bypass barriers for resolving conflicts. There are "classic" barriers that appear again and again in almost any negotiating process. A map of these barriers and relevant insights to cope with them can improve the ability of mediators and negotiators to discover key game changers. My colleagues and I are working on this project.

Four Variables

This book introduces a powerful instrument for relationship building and conflict resolution—the Solution-Focused Negotiation. It is an effective tool to cope with conflicts and tensions in various dimensions of our social life—from family disputes to international politics. The initiative rests on three pillars: Transformation—turning opposing parties into a negotiation cooperative; Practicality—focusing on pragmatic solutions to a resolvable (negotiable) problem; and Discovery—finding key game changers.

The product of an effective and efficient negotiating process (a combination of these three elements) is a pragmatic and innovative negotiation cooperative. This configuration creates **M**otivation and commitment to the process, provides **R**ules for pragmatic talks and offers a platform for controlling **E**motions and discovering new **I**deas.

In conclusion, this book shows that the ability of opposing parties to successfully conclude Solution-Focused Negotiation is a function of four variables: **Motivation** to resolve the conflict by peaceful means, **Rules** for constructive dialogue, **Emotional** control and **Ideas** that promote solutions.

Let me present the major challenges to a successful Solution-Focused Negotiation by introducing the Mediator's Trap. It can be a good introduction to a more detailed analysis of the structure, mechanism and operation of this powerful negotiating instrument.

Notes

1. Lax and Sebenius (1992) used this term but presented the dilemma slightly differently.
2. https://www.merriam-webster.com/words-at-play/pyrrhic-victory-meaning.
3. See Hassner (2003).
4. Visit http://mindsofpeace.org/.
5. See Duhigg (2012).
6. Mitchell (1999, 25–29).

References

Duhigg, Charles. 2012. *The power of habit: Why we do what we do in life and business.* New York: Random House.
Hassner, Ron E. 2003. "To Halve and to Hold": Conflicts over Sacred Space and the Problem of Indivisibility. *Security Studies*, 12 (4): 1–33.
Lax, David A. & Sebenius, James K. 1992. The manager as negotiator: The negotiator's dilemma: Creating and claiming value. *Dispute resolution*, 2: 49–62.
Mitchell, George John. 1999. *Making Peace.* New York, NY: Alfred A. Knopf.

3

The Mediator's Trap
Success and Failure of Solution-Focused Negotiation

Why do negotiations fail when mediators believe they should succeed? And, why do negotiations succeed when mediators believe they are probably going to fail?

A major reason for such miscalculation is an improper assessment of the situation by mediators. In the first case (expected success—actual failure), the mediator believes that the major barriers for conflict resolution are tactical, while, in fact, they are strategic. In the second case (expected failure and actual success), the mediator believes the main barriers are strategic, while, in fact, they are only tactical. I suggest labeling this type of miscalculation "the Mediator's Trap".

This chapter clarifies the difference between tactical and strategic barriers for reaching a negotiated agreement of mutual benefit. It demonstrates that inappropriate assessment—a confusion between tactical and strategic barriers—can lead to the Mediator's Trap in almost any type of negotiating interaction, from family disputes to politics.

This chapter describes and analyzes a classic case in the history of Solution-Focused Negotiation—the 1978 Camp David Summit. In the Camp David Summit, US President Jimmy Carter brokered historic peace agreements between two bitter enemies, Egyptian President Anwar Sadat and Israeli Prime Minister Menachem Begin. It was a turning point in the history of one of the most difficult conflicts in the world—the Arab–Israeli confrontation.

The Arab–Israeli conflict is a classic case of intractable conflict. It is a long-time violent struggle that seems to resist any form of resolution. It is like a chronic disease that controls the body. The 1978 Camp David Summit, which brought peace between Egypt and Israel, is a signpost in the confrontation. It changed the structure of the conflict and created a sharp turn in the history and politics of the Middle East.

However, analysis indicates that President Carter wrongly identified the tactical and strategic barriers and this error produced unnecessary social costs. The lesson is that a powerful mediator—an intermediary with political, economic and military leverage—can fall victim to his own power.

Intractable Conflict—An Unending Story

Intractable conflict is a protracted, violent and long-term struggle, wherein generation after generation is born into a reality of fear, intimidation and aggression. Intractable conflict can appear and develop around various issues and values encompassing almost any dimension of our social life. Intractable conflict can be a power struggle between super powers who can quite easily destroy the world (the Cold War); it can be a religious conflict between different factions about the proper way to worship God (Catholics versus Protestants); and it can be a bitter struggle for freedom, equity and democracy (the battle against the Apartheid system in South Africa). Most cases of intractable conflict are conceived as existential to the conflicting parties.

The different types of intractable conflict share one major characteristic—they are longtime struggles that resist almost any type of peaceful resolution. The story of almost any intractable conflict is like a work of art, a drama. Their narratives have a preface, an introduction, different chapters, developments, tensions and twists in the main plot. But intractable conflicts, unlike works of art, do not have an end.[1] The Arab–Israeli conflict is a classic case of intractable conflict.

Jewish Israelis have believed that the establishment of Israel is an existential need. They saw in building a national home for Jews as the only way to cope with the ongoing history of antisemitism, persecution and discrimination, which culminated in the Jews' biggest disaster—the Holocaust. In contrast, the Arab countries saw the establishment of Israel as another instance of imperialist exploitation and colonization by the West, which caused them suffering, misery and humiliation.

A pivotal player in the Arab–Israeli confrontation was Egypt, the strongest Arab country in the region. Since the establishment of Israel in 1948 until the peace treaty in 1979, Egypt and Israel were officially in a state of war. The relationship between Egypt and Israel started with violence, aggression and fear.

3 The Mediator's Trap

One of the turning points in the confrontation was the Six Day War in 1967. Israel faced a coalition of three Arab countries—Egypt, Syria and Jordan. The armies of the rival countries met in the battlefield. Israel survived and demonstrated to the Arab world that it will be almost impossible to dismantle the Jewish state by force. Israel succeeded to expand its territory and establish more defensible borders.

In the south, Israel took over (occupied) the Sinai Peninsula, a very important area for Egypt. It is one of the most beautiful places in the world and has natural resources, such as oil fields. Egyptians believe that the Sinai Peninsula has belonged to them since ancient times.

Anwar Sadat, the President of Egypt, was determined to restore the Sinai Peninsula to Egypt by all means. In contrast, Israelis saw the area as a military strategic asset and rejected the idea of giving it back to Egypt. Diplomatic attempts by the Egyptians to recover the loss to Egypt failed. As a result, Sadat followed the proclamation of the famous military theorist, Carl von Clausewitz—war is "the continuation of politics by other means". He decided to use force.

In October 1973, the armies of Egypt and Syria launched a surprise attack on Israel. Israel was in a grave danger for its existence. The Egyptian army succeeded in regaining control over the Sinai Peninsula and its forces were on the road to Tel-Aviv.

Israel managed to survive. It pushed back the Arab armies. The Israeli army recovered the area that was captured during the Six Day War, including the Sinai Peninsula. The cost of the war was horrible for all sides.

The 1973 war demonstrated the intensity and intractability of the Arab–Israeli conflict. Israel and Egypt suffered severe human losses. Achieving peace between the two countries seemed to be an impossible mission.

Israelis, who live in profound fear for their existence, were not willing to endanger their security. The conventional wisdom in Israel was—for security reasons—it is better to hold the Sinai Peninsula without peace than to have peace without this area. In contrast, Egyptians demanded restoration of the Sinai Peninsula to Egypt as a precondition to any conflict resolution effort. Diplomatic attempts to broker peace between the two antagonists failed.

In 1977, Anwar Sadat, the leader of the strongest Arab country and the most rigidly entrenched of Israel's enemies, surprised the world. He declared his intension to come to Jerusalem to talk about peace in the Israeli parliament, the Knesset. Menachem Begin, the Israeli Prime Minister, invited him (or, more precisely, did not have any choice but to accept Sadat's self-invitation). Sadat's astonishing visit to Jerusalem in 1977 was the beginning of a turning point in Middle Eastern politics in general and the Arab–Israeli conflict in particular.

Sadat's astonishing visit to Jerusalem and his brilliant speech in the Israeli parliament was a game changer. It enabled the parties to engage in a Solution-Focused Negotiation under the mediation of an intermediary with power and leverage, the US President, Jimmy Carter. However, bringing the antagonist leaders to the negotiating table was not enough to conclude a peace agreement, to say the very least.

The engagement of politically entrenched antagonists in a Solution-Focused Negotiation is a major step forward in the long road to change. However, it does not guarantee success. The history of political negotiations shows that peace initiatives, especially in difficult cases of intractable conflict, are in constant risk of collapsing. The negotiations can fail and the situation can deteriorate again into another cycle of violence. Such a tragic outcome can emerge even if the mediator has as much political, economic and military leverage as the President of the US.

In difficult situations of intractable conflict, key game changers are needed to begin, support and successfully conclude Solution-Focused Negotiations.

Barriers and Game Changers

Conflict is an unpleasant situation. Often enough, it is quite clear to conflicting parties that a negotiated solution to their struggle is better than the status quo. However, it still can be an enormous task to engage them in a Solution-Focused Negotiation. There are psychological and substantive barriers to conflict resolution.

Barriers to meeting around the negotiating table are multidimensional. For example, the opposing parties do not trust one another, they believe that the conflict is irresolvable, and they are insecure in their negotiating capabilities. In difficult situations of intractable conflict—such as the Arab–Israeli confrontation—the intensity of the barriers is very high and the gravity of the situation is much more severe than typical conflicts.

In situations of intractable conflict, the parties see the confrontation as an existential threat. Each party believes in the inhumanity of the other side. They are afraid of the outcomes of any peacemaking initiative. A game changer is required to bypass barriers to conflict resolution in order to engage the parties in Solution-Focused Negotiation.

The dramatic and astonishing visit of Sadat to Jerusalem was a game changer. It enabled the entrenched antagonists to come to the negotiating table. However, the story of the peace process between Egypt and Israel demonstrates that bringing the parties to the negotiating table does not guarantee success. It is only the beginning of an exhausting and difficult journey to peace. The parties face multiple barriers to reaching agreements and the negotiation can be in constant danger of collapsing.

Barriers around the negotiating table are also multidimensional. Examples:

- Positional bargaining—the negotiators show inflexibility and remain entrenched in their initial positions.
- Dissonance in communication—the parties interpret messages according to their biased conceptions and do not listen constructively to each other.
- Lack of knowledge—the parties do not know how to cope with major substantial problems and settle their differences.

Key game changers are needed to bypass barriers at the negotiating table and to progress toward agreements.

In order to bring peace and stability in situations of deep-rooted conflict, the mission to involve the parties in constructive Solution-Focused Negotiation is multidimensional. There are barriers and obstacles at each stage of the process. The first challenge is to bring the parties to the negotiating table and guarantee their commitment to the process. The next challenge is to keep the process alive and to ensure constructive and pragmatic talks. The concluding challenge is to successfully finalize the negotiating process by motivating the parties to conclude agreements of mutual benefit.[2] Success at each stage requires key game changers.

Sadat's drastic and dramatic initiative—coming to Jerusalem to talk peace in the Israeli parliament—was a major game changer that enabled the initiation of a peace process. It paved the way to engage entrenched enemies in intensive Solution-Focused Negotiation. But it was not enough to bring peace to the Middle East. A mediator with leverage entered the picture to lead the negotiation.

Following Sadat's unilateral move, the President of the US, Jimmy Carter, decided to lead the peace process. He invited the Egyptian and Israeli leaders, Sadat and Begin, to 13 days of Solution-Focused Negotiation at an isolated location—Camp David.

The story of the historic 1978 Camp David Summit is a classic case in the history of political negotiation. It can serve as a laboratory for the study of Solution-Focused Negotiation. That summit demonstrates the challenges of political negotiation and mediation.

At first glance, it looked like the dramatic effect of Sadat's visit to Jerusalem led Sadat and Begin to reach the point of no return in the journey for peace. Carter seemed to believe it would be relatively easy to broker a peace agreement between the two leaders. In reality, the negotiations were very difficult and the summit was on the brink of collapse. Carter described the negotiating accords—which he expected to be calm, friendly and relatively easy—as one of the most difficult and frustrating initiatives in his lifetime.[3]

The dissonance between Carter's expectations (relatively easy process) and reality (very difficult negotiation) indicates that Jimmy Carter—the President of the US—fell into the Mediator's Trap. His assessment of the negotiating challenges seems to have been mistaken. He seems to have confused the strategic and tactical barriers.

Strategic and Tactical Barriers

We can assume that adversaries agree to participate in Solution-Focused Negotiation because they hope to improve their situation. They believe it is possible to achieve a peaceful resolution to the conflict that is better than the status quo. However, the willingness of the participants (mediator and negotiators) to take part in an intensive negotiating process does not guarantee success. There are barriers and obstacles that can sabotage the interaction and bring it to a dead-end or to an unexpected destructive outcome.

To better understand the challenge of Solution-Focused Negotiation, I suggest distinguishing between two categories of barriers—strategic and tactical. A *strategic barrier* is a strong motivation of participants (mediator and/or negotiators) to block any possibility to reach agreements of mutual advantage. For example, negotiating with someone who is not authorized to make decisions and has to follow uncompromised policy can be a waste of valuable time and energy.

A *tactical barrier* is a problem in the actual interaction that creates an obstacle to reaching an agreement of mutual benefit. For example, the use of provocations at the negotiating table can create hostility, anger and distrust.

Metaphorically speaking, *strategic barriers* are external to the negotiating table, while *tactical barriers* are obstacles at the negotiating table. Strategic and tactical barriers to reach negotiated agreements can emerge in almost any kind of negotiation, from family disputes to politics. However, it is quite easy to demonstrate their destructive operation in situations of complex negotiation.

3 The Mediator's Trap

In 2021, a crisis emerged in the education system in Israel. Conflict erupted between the teachers' union and the Ministry of Finance. The leader of the teachers' union demanded a substantial raise in the salary of the teachers. The representatives of the Ministry of Finance rejected the demand. They demanded major reforms in the Israeli education system as a precondition for any discussion about a salary raise. The parties reached a deadlock. The impression was that the situation is going to deteriorate into an inevitable long teachers' strike.

Suddenly—without any warning—"breaking news" changed the negotiating game. News agencies reported that the leader of the teachers' union is a devoted member of the main opposition party (Likud) at that time. The practical meaning was that there is a strategic barrier to resolving the conflict around the negotiating table.

At that time, the opposition parties in the Israeli parliament did everything they could to overthrow the government. Its members swore to reject and object to any position, action and initiative—justified or unjustified—of the government. Their intention was to create chaos that eventually will lead to the fall of the government. The news implied that it was expected from the leader of the teachers' union—who, according to the news, was a devoted member of the main opposition party—to follow the opposition policy and sabotage the negotiation by blocking any possibility to reach an agreement.

According to the news, the loyalty of the leader of the teachers' union to her political party (the opposition) was higher than her loyalty to the teachers. It was claimed that she betrayed her role to protect the interests of the teachers and did not negotiate in good faith. In other words, the news revealed a strategic barrier to conflict resolution—an incentive outside of the negotiating table that motivates one party (the leader of the teachers' union) to behave destructively at the negotiating table.

The news started a war in the media between the two parties. The representatives of the Ministry of Finance accused the leader of the teachers' union in betraying her job as the representative of the union. They claimed that she is operating against the interests of the pupils, teachers and parents. In contrast, the leader of the union tried to defend her public credibility and reputation. She accused the representatives of the Ministry of Finance of orchestrating an aggressive campaign against her integrity in order to sabotage her efforts to defend the interests of the teachers and resolve the conflict. She claimed that they spread fake news in order to weaken her position at the negotiating table.

The blame game in the media (outside the negotiating table) created a hostile atmosphere at the negotiating table. The accusation of a strategic barrier (the leader of the teachers' union has a conflict of interest) also created tactical barriers, such as a hostile relationship at the table. In this complicated situation, any intermediary can, quite easily, fall in the Mediator's Trap.

If the news were correct, the commitment of the leader of the teacher's union to the opposition party created a strategic barrier to any negotiation. Any mediator—who was not aware of this critical piece of information—would have probably fallen in the Mediator's Trap. The mediator could believe that the difficulties to reach an agreement are due to tactical barriers (lack of trust and hostile relationships) without noticing that there is a major strategic barrier to resolve: the union leader's conflict of interest.

This crisis demonstrates the complexity of negotiation and the multidimensional challenge of mediation. Each party had to negotiate with multiple groups. On one level, each side negotiated solutions to the conflict with the other around the negotiating table. On other levels, each one of them needed to negotiate its position with its audiences, which included teachers, parents and the Israeli public.

The negotiation with these various audiences—outside the negotiating table—worked in two different directions. On the one hand, each party needed to demonstrate to its audiences that it protects their best interests. On the other hand, each party needed to prepare its audiences for solutions that require concessions and costs. How can a human mediator cope with such complexity and lead the parties to reach a satisfactory deal of multidimensional advantage?

We can identify two key game changers that, eventually, enabled this conflict to be resolved. The first game changer was timing. The crisis between the parties reached its peak during the summer vacation. The holiday was about to end. The Israeli public, especially the parents, were exhausted from the Corona crisis. It would have been extremely difficult for families to tolerate a strike in the education system. The opposing parties knew that if the crisis will continue and the teachers will strike, they will have to provide very good explanations for their inability to resolve the conflict.

The second game changer was political. The Israeli government resigned. This led to an early general election. The opposing parties could not afford a teachers' strike during the election period. The Minister of Finance, who is a political leader, and the leader of the teachers' union, who was identified as a member of the main opposition party (Likud), knew very well that a teachers' strike could have a negative impact on Israeli voters. As one would expect, the two sides tried to save face and show that they are protecting the interests of their audiences until the last minute. The parties reached an agreement one day before the beginning of the new school year.

Jimmy Carter, the President of the US, tried to eliminate strategic barriers to conflict resolution. He invited Sadat and Begin to participate in a Solution-Focused Negotiation at Camp David. Camp David is an isolated place. By "imprisoning" the parties, Carter hoped to broker a deal in three or four days.

The political theorist Eytan Gilboa argues that the Camp David Summit is a classic case of 'closed-door diplomacy'. The media and the public were partially excluded from the talks. Everyone knew that negotiations were taking place at Camp David. But, no one, except the summit participants and their inner circle of advisors, knew what was happening around the negotiating table. The content of the talks was hidden from the media and the public.[4]

The "imprisoning" of the parties at an isolated place (Camp David) and the efforts to keep the content of the talks secret was not a coincidence. The intention was to eliminate strategic barriers, such as political pressure from outside sources and public statements by Sadat and Begin that would commit them to rigid and inflexible positions in the negotiation. Did the President of the US—a mediator with political, economic and military power—succeed in eliminating strategic barriers to conflict resolution?

Perhaps, these were the initial thoughts of Jimmy Carter. In retrospect, this belief might be a result of his own self-deception.

The Trap of a Problem-Solving Mediator—Competition and Cooperation

It is quite common for mediators (especially, mediators with leverage and experience) to believe in their magical powers. They are quite confident that they can craft a deal even in very difficult cases. However, quite often, they are not sufficiently familiar with the disputing parties and they are not fully aware of certain aspects of the adversaries' political views, motivations and impediments. These elements can have an important influence on the behavior of the disputing parties at the negotiating table. It looks like this was the situation of Jimmy Carter, the President of the US at the 1978 Camp David Summit.

Sadat's dramatic visit to Jerusalem, which can be viewed as a diplomatic offensive against a hardline Israeli government, was not enough to create a change. The parties were far from reaching a deal. The active intervention of a mediator was required to use the momentum of that astonishing visit to broker a peace agreement. Jimmy Carter, the President of the US (a mediator with political and economic leverage) invited Begin and Sadat for thirteen days of Solution-Focused Negotiation at an isolated place—Camp David.

The classical literature on international negotiation distinguishes three types of negotiation: bargaining, problem-solving and consensus-building. Each negotiation type requires a different type of mediator. A mediator with leverage can be effective in leading a bargaining process—a competitive form of negotiation. A problem-solving facilitator has the qualifications to engage adversaries in a cooperative problem-solving process[5]—a joint search for agreements that address the interests, needs and fears of both parties. And a coalition-builder intermediary can be useful in building consensus—establishing a broad active support for a peace settlement.

The Camp David Accord of 1978 took place in the Cold War era. Realism was the dominant paradigm in the study of international relations. Classical realists emphasize the competitive aspect of negotiation—negotiation as bargaining. Accordingly, one would expect the President of the US to act as a power mediator who leads a competitive bargaining process. However, Carter's memoirs indicate that he had a different plan.

Carter, who has scientific knowledge and education, believed that the two parties (Sadat and Begin) had reached the point of no return. He assumed that the two leaders have strong incentives and motivations to reach a peace deal. He approached the situation as an engineer that needed to solve a problem.

Carter's initial mediation strategy was to explore the needs and fears of each side and craft a deal that they will not be able to resist. Unfortunately, he was not aware of a strategic barrier that guided the behavior of the two sides and made the negotiation almost impossible. Carter, who later would describe the summit as a frustrating experience, could not even imagine the magnitude of the challenge and the difficulties he was about to face.

Begin and Sadat held different visions of the desired peace process. Sadat advocated a comprehensive peace process between Israel and the Arab states. Begin advocated a separate peace process between Israel and Egypt. These different viewpoints were based, at least partly, on strategic considerations and external pressures.

Sadat wished to break the isolation of Egypt from the Arab world, which followed his unilateral initiative. A comprehensive peace process between Israel and the Arab world had the potential to achieve this goal. Sadat seemed to believe that 'the Palestinian Problem' is the gate to achieve a comprehensive peace. In his historic speech in the Israeli parliament, Sadat repeatedly emphasized that there is not going to be peace in the Middle East without solving the Palestinian Problem—"As for the Palestinians' cause, nobody could deny that it is the crux of the entire problem ... the Palestinian problem is the core and essence of the conflict and that, so long as it continues to be unresolved, the conflict will continue to aggravate, reaching new dimensions. In all sincerity, I tell you that there can be no peace without the Palestinians".[6]

Begin, a hardliner champion of Greater Israel, did not want to negotiate solutions to the Palestinian problem with Sadat. He was not ready to discuss concessions in the West Bank and Jerusalem. He demonstrated his position with actions. As a reaction to Carter's request to stop expanding the Jewish settlement project, the Israeli government recognized new Jewish settlements in the West Bank as permanent.[7]

It is common knowledge that continuing to settle Jews in the West Bank and Gaza—which Palestinians see as their own land—is a death verdict to any peace process between Israelis and Palestinians. Begin's political move seemed to be a clear message to Carter and Sadat before the Camp David Accords began—the Palestinian problem is not on the negotiating table. Carter—who was furious due to Begin's political move—did not take the message seriously. He still believed that a problem-solving facilitation is the best way to lead the negotiation between the Egyptian and Israeli leaders.

The difference between Sadat's and Begin's viewpoints on the desired peace process constituted a strategic barrier that stalled the negotiations and soured the relationship between them. As a desperate choice, Carter, who started the negotiations as a problem-solving facilitator, turned into a power mediator. He used the political and economic leverage of the US to compel the parties to reach a peace deal. The President of the US separated the negotiators and met individually with each one of them to discuss the main issues. The shuttle negotiation enabled him to efficiently use his leverage as the President of a Super Power. He used the political and economic abilities of the US—threats and generous offers of financial support—to push the two leaders to reach an agreement.

Can it be that Carter's initial assessment—that Sadat and Begin reached the point of no return—was completely wrong? Had Carter actually controlled and manipulated the situation? Or, perhaps, someone else manipulated him?

The Trap of a Power Mediator: Who is the "Real" Manipulator?

In the previous section, I showed that Carter, who started as a problem-solving facilitator, ended as a power mediator. He used political and economic leverage to compel two antagonists to reach an agreement. Is this analysis correct? Had Carter actually controlled and led the negotiating interaction? Can it be that the President of the US missed something?

Negotiating partners, like almost all human beings, are complex creatures who live in a dynamic environment. They have various interests in multiple dimensions. They have interests that can lead to clashes and they have interests that can lead to cooperation. For example, a couple in a divorce process, who negotiate the division of their property, often have conflicting interests. On the one hand, each one of them wishes to gain a larger part of their property for selfish reasons (competitive motivation). On the other hand, they have a strong motivation to peacefully settle the dispute for the benefit of their children (cooperative motivation).

Scholars of negotiation taught us that the ambivalence between competition and cooperation creates a dilemma that is often labeled 'the Negotiator's Dilemma'. Negotiators need to choose between competitive and cooperative strategies.[8] Did Sadat and Begin face a Negotiator's Dilemma?

We saw the different interests of Begin (separate peace) and Sadat (comprehensive peace). These competitive motivations soured their relationship and had the potential to cause the Camp David negotiation to fail. However, this is only part of the picture.

The three leaders involved in the Camp David Accords—Sadat, Begin and Carter—also had a shared interest—a strong motivation to bring the summit to success. Therefore, it is reasonable to assume that Carter's assessment at the beginning of the summit—that the peace process had reached the point of no return—was correct. Let us analyze the compatible motivations of the three leaders—Sadat, Begin and Carter—to bring the Camp David Accords to a successful conclusion.

Sadat, who challenged the very existence of Israel in the 1973 war, did not abandon his desire to return the Sinai Peninsula to Egyptian control and was looking for an opportunity to establish a strong relationship with the US. Moreover, after his bold peacemaking visit to Jerusalem, returning to Egypt without a deal would have seriously damaged his prestige at home and in the Arab world.

Sadat's drastic initiative had such an impact on the international community, in general, and on the Israeli public, in particular, that Begin—a longtime advocate of Greater Israel—also could not afford the summit to end without a deal. There were good chances that coming back to Israel without an agreement would have caused Begin and his government to lose credibility among the Israeli people and to face a serious confrontation with the US. Indeed, for Carter, the President of the US, failure was not an option. It would have seriously sabotaged his political career and damaged the prestige of the US as the leading superpower.

In short, Sadat and Begin understood that they could not allow the negotiations to fail. The tough bargaining helped them to "motivate" Carter—who was caught in the same trap—to increase his generous financial offers. Following the agreement, both sides (Israel and Egypt) were to receive massive economic and military aid from the US. Israel was to receive $3 billion in military and financial assistance; Egypt was to receive $2 billion in military equipment. This was in addition to the existing 1979 foreign aid allocation of $1.8 billion to Israel and $1 billion to Egypt.[9]

According to our analysis, Sadat and Begin negotiated in at least three dimensions. First, they negotiated the terms of the peace agreement with each other. Second, each one of them negotiated the price that the US is willing to pay for a peace treaty with Carter. Third, each negotiator, Sadat and Begin, negotiated with himself major issues that could have influenced his strategy and actions at the negotiating table. Examples:

"Should I stay committed to my initial position?"
"Which concessions would be accepted by the public?"
"Where is the balance between saving face and compromising?"

It is difficult to know if our assumption that Sadat and Begin manipulated Carter (indirectly bargaining the "price" of a peace treaty) is true, partly true or completely false. However, the analysis has a lesson. Mediators, especially mediators with leverage and strong interests, should be very careful to not become victims of their own power and ambition.

Handling the different motivations of the parties is only one challenging element in a complicated conflict resolution puzzle. There were genuine difficult problems that needed to be addressed by the negotiators. Political pressure and economic gifts were not enough to bring the parties to conclude agreements that could bring peace to the region.

We can identity at least two more elements that could help the parties reach a peace deal—'Islands of Agreement' and knowledge about the future solution to the conflict.

'Islands of Agreement'—Points of Agreement Within Disagreements

Leading negotiations can be a difficult task. A mediator, who, often enough, does not know the parties, is taking responsibility for guiding them in a difficult and complicated journey. He involves them in a joint search for a satisfactory solution to their conflict. The mediator has to make important decisions—such as, choosing a process strategy, an issue strategy and a timing strategy—in a situation of uncertainty. Quite often, a third-party mediator does not know the motivations, interests, needs and barriers of the disputing parties.

The point of departure in our analysis is that Sadat and Begin—who agreed to participate in the Camp David Accords—held contrasting views on the desired peace process. Sadat advocated a comprehensive peace process in the Middle East. He believed that the Palestinian problem is the key to achieve it. Begin advocated a separate peace between Egypt and Israel without any discussion on the Palestinian problem. How does one create balance between these different demands? How does one address the interests and needs of the opposing parties simultaneously? How does one conclude a peace treaty of mutual benefit?

Any negotiation requires a joint basis for discussion, a common ground. Indeed, a careful analysis reveals issues that could be mutually agreed by both sides. The two leaders seem to have points of agreement within their disagreements, which Gabriella Blum labeled 'Islands of Agreement'.

Begin could agree with Sadat on two main issues: A comprehensive peace in the Middle East is desirable and the Palestinian problem is not going to vanish or be resolved by itself. Sadat could agree with Begin that a peace contract between Egypt and Israel is desirable and necessary. These 'Islands of Agreement'—points of agreement within their disagreements—enabled them to meet at the negotiating table, keep the process alive in times of crisis and explore different solutions to their conflict. However, identifying 'Islands of Agreement' was not enough to bring the process to a successful conclusion.

Identifying 'Islands of Agreement' can be an important element in the efforts to initiate, maintain and lead constructive negotiation. As I am going to show in Chap. 7, it enables the parties to discover negotiable differences. But still, it is not enough to conclude agreements.

The irony of fate is that, often enough, tough negotiating partners know the solution to their conflict already at the beginning of the process. It seems that this was the case of Sadat and Begin.

Negotiators Know the Solutions at the Beginning of the Process

Scholars of negotiation taught us that opposing parties—locked in a frustrating conflict—have various needs and interests. Analyzing the needs, fears and interests of the parties can invite creative ideas that have the potential to illuminate the negotiated problem in a different light. However, often enough, it seems that, deep in their minds, the parties already know the solutions to their conflict before the negotiation starts.

In many difficult cases of conflict, it seems that the solution is already written on the wall. However, the parties refuse, are afraid or are not ready to see it. This tragic phenomenon appears in almost all kinds of conflict—from family disputes to international politics.

The parents of my daughter's friend wanted to get a divorce. The relationship was very bad. They could not reach a divorce agreement by themselves. They met in a courtroom to settle their differences.

In the first meeting, the judge sketched general outlines of a divorce agreement. He told them that they have two options: to accept the deal or to reach a similar deal after one year of expensive litigation. The judge explained and emphasized that the trial process will cost them at least $300,000 in lawyers' fees.

Unfortunately, the couple did not accept the advice of the judge. As the judge predicted, after a year of expensive, frustrating and exhausting litigation, they reached a similar deal. They paid about $300,000 to their lawyers. In political conflicts, the stakes can be much higher and the cost to society can be much more tragic.

'The Troubles' in Northern Ireland were considered to be one of the most entrenched conflicts in the world. In 1973, political elites of different sides reached a peace deal in the village of Sunningdale, England. The Sunningdale initiative collapsed into another dark cycle of violence and despair after a few months. The Good Friday Agreement of 1998, which symbolized the end of 'The Troubles', was quite similar to the Sunningdale Agreement of 1973. It took the rival parties 26 years of fighting, violence and bloodshed, and two years of difficult negotiations to accept a peace pact based on the same previously negotiated principles and guidelines.

The new chapter in the history of Northern Ireland, which started in 1998, was based on the negotiated framework for peace and stability that had already been reached in 1973. The Irish politician, Seamus Mallon, ironically described the "Good Friday Agreement" as "Sunningdale for slow learners".

It seems that Sadat and Begin already knew (at least in the back of their minds) the final outcome of the summit at the beginning of the negotiations. Sadat, who emphasized the necessity to solve the Palestinian Problem, did not invite Palestinian representatives to participate in the Camp David Accords. Israel, even under the leadership of Begin, did not utilize the great tourism potential of Sinai Peninsula and most of the area remained uncultivated. However, these hopeful signs did not guarantee a successful negotiation.

The parties still needed a key game changer to overcome the strategic barrier—different viewpoints on the desired peace process (comprehensive peace versus separate peace) that stalled the negotiation and threaten to be a deal breaker.

The Game Changer

The analysis indicates that each negotiator in the Camp David Accords had competing motivations that pushed the negotiation in different directions. On the one hand, the parties faced a strategic barrier—different viewpoints on the desired peace process and its outcomes—and a tactical barrier—Sadat and Begin detested one another. On the other hand, both of them could not afford the summit to fail. They shared points of agreement within their disagreement ('Islands of Agreement'), and they knew—in the back of their mind—the outline of a possible peace pact. To overcome the deadlock, they needed a game changer.

The psychologist Herbert Kelman claimed that negotiation is a joint search for "an agreement that addresses the fundamental needs and fears of both parties on a basis of reciprocity".[10] In this case, the key game changer that enabled them to overcome the strategic barrier was the idea to conclude two agreements. Each agreement addressed the needs and interests of one party in a way that the other party could not reject. The two agreements created a balance between their different and contrasting interests, needs and fears.

The Camp David summit ended with two agreements: "Framework for Peace in the Middle East" and "Framework for the Conclusion of a Peace Treaty between Egypt and Israel". The first sketched principles for peace between Israel and the Arab world, and offered a road map for resolving the Palestinian Problem (Sadat's position). The second specified principles for a peace treaty between Egypt and Israel (Begin's position).

Did the Camp David Accords indeed succeed in bridging the gap between the visions of Sadat and Begin (a strategic barrier) and what was the cost?

The First Agreement and the Strategic Mistake

The first agreement—"Framework for Peace in the Middle East"—became the basis for almost all subsequent peace agreements between Israelis and Palestinians, such as the Oslo Accords of 1993. Egypt and Israel agreed on the necessity to provide full autonomy to the inhabitants in "the West Bank and Gaza for a period not exceeding five years. ... As soon as possible, but not later than the third year after the beginning of the transitional period, negotiations will take place to determine the final status of the West Bank and Gaza and its relationship with its neighbors, and to conclude a peace treaty between Israel and Jordan by the end of the transitional period. These negotiations will be conducted among Egypt, Israel, Jordan, and the elected representatives of the inhabitants of the West Bank and Gaza".[11]

This agreement suggests a practical program to implement Sadat's vision of a comprehensive peace. It sketches a road map for solving the Palestinian Problem as a necessary step to create a momentum for peace between Israel and its Arab neighbors. Did Begin relinquish his demand to focus only on negotiating peace between Egypt and Israel (a separate peace)? Did the Accords succeed in neutralizing the political forces that motivated Begin, at the beginning of the process, to reject any discussion of the Palestinian Problem? Was it possible to implement the program that this agreement suggested?

The Camp David Accords did not bring a comprehensive peace to the Middle East. It did not succeed in overcoming the strategic barriers that Begin had at the beginning of the process. Perhaps Begin changed part of his worldview during the negotiating process. But his main supporters were (mentally) in a different place. They did not participate in Solution-Focused Negotiation and the process did not raise doubts in their ideology and worldview. Begin was under intense political pressure. It was clearly expressed in the Likud (Begin's political party) response to the Camp David Agreements.

Begin's supporters accepted the idea of autonomy for the Palestinians. However, they used a kind of "Talmudic sophistication" to interpret the concept "autonomy". They claimed that Israel's position is autonomy for the people and not autonomy for the land. In the Likud response to the Camp David treaty, it repeatedly specified that "The right of the Jewish people to Eretz Israel is an eternal one. ... The autonomy arrangements agreed upon at Camp David are [a] guarantee that under no circumstances will a 'Palestinian' State be established in part of Western Eretz Israel".

One of the practical meanings is that "Settlements in the Land of Israel is a right and an integral part of the nation's security".[12] They decided to continue the Jewish settlement project in the West Bank, which is a major obstacle to any effort to find a negotiated formula to divide the land between Israelis and Palestinians ('Two State Solution').

One result of the inability to create momentum for a comprehensive peace process in the Middle East, while achieving a separate peace treaty between Egypt and Israel, was the Palestinization of the Arab–Israeli conflict. Palestinization of the Arab–Israeli conflict made the Palestinians the central player in the confrontation. The 1979 peace treaty between Israel and Egypt contributed to this tendency which started after the 1967 war. On the one hand, Arab leaders who would not go to war with Israel claimed that Palestinians have the responsibility to dismantle the Jewish state. On the other hand, the Palestinians themselves understood that they had to take their fate in their own hands.

The Camp David Accords demonstrate the power of Solution-Focused Negotiation as a deal-making instrument. The initiative can be very effective in leading entrenched antagonists to reach settlements. However, it also concertizes the limitations of this conflict resolution tool.

It seems that Begin—the hardliner—changed his position in regard to the Palestinian problem as a result of the interaction. This quite drastic change made him negotiate conditions for a comprehensive peace and reach an agreement. But, his traditional supporters were not ready for such a change.

The strategic mistake of President Carter—a mediator with leverage—was to negotiate the "Framework for Peace in the Middle East" with the wrong players. Begin and Sadat were not able to bring peace and stability to the Middle East by themselves, even with the support of the US. The intensive negotiations in Camp David were not enough to bring peace between Israel and its neighbors.

The ambitious project of a comprehensive peace in the Middle East is a peacemaking revolution that requires a multifaceted approach to conflict resolution. A multidimensional process suggests dealing with the confrontation from different sides, directions and dimensions. It requires operating different (competing and complementary) peacemaking channels—such as political-elite diplomacy, public diplomacy and people-to-people diplomacy—in parallel.[13]

Different diplomatic settings have different roles and goals. Political-elite diplomacy offers diplomatic channels for a wide circle of political leaders and elites to negotiate peace agreements. People-to-people diplomacy provides instruments to establish peacemaking coalitions at the grassroots level and prepare the people for change. Public diplomacy creates peacemaking links between leaders and people.

Public diplomacy operates in two different directions—top-down and bottom-up. On the one hand, public diplomacy offers tools (such as public relations, advertising and marketing) for leaders to prepare the people for peace agreements and getting their feedback on new ideas for a peaceful social order (top-down). On the other hand, public diplomacy provides instruments (such as social protest and demonstrations) for the people to motivate their leaders to initiate a peacemaking policy and conclude agreements (bottom-up).

A multifaceted approach to conflict resolution is necessary and useful in situations, like the Israeli-Palestinian struggle, where ordinary people, and not standing armies, are at the center of the confrontation. The intention is to involve the different elements of the opposing societies—leaders, elites and ordinary people—in the struggle for change. Such a comprehensive strategy was not necessary to broker peace between Egypt and Israel, but it is critical for the peacemaking efforts in the Israeli-Palestinian case.

There is a big difference between the Israeli-Palestinian conflict and the Egyptian-Israeli struggle. Israel and Egypt are established states with functioning institutions. It was possible for the leaders—Sadat and Begin—to conclude peace agreements that could be implemented and kept. The Israeli-Palestinian struggle is a different kind of intractable conflict. In this conflict, ordinary citizens are at the front line of daily confrontations and the possibilities to keep order and stability in transitional periods are much more limited.

Perhaps, engaging state leaders (Sadat and Begin) in a Solution-Focused Negotiation that excluded the media and the public was the only effective way to conclude peace agreements. However, it was not enough to solve the Israeli-Palestinian conflict. And, it was certainly not enough to bring peace and stability to the Middle East.

The Camp David Accords involved only Sadat and Begin in the negotiation for a comprehensive peace in the Middle East. President Carter, the US mediator, did not show any effort to bring other pivotal players—such as the Palestinians—to the negotiating table. The questions are: Why? Is it only the result of Carter's miscalculations? Did the US President over estimate his power?

The Camp David Accords of 1978 took place in the Cold War era. At that time, the dominant paradigm in international relations was Realism. Classical Realists interpret a conflict situation in terms of a power struggle between competing interests. Their key assumptions are: States are the dominant actors that dictate world order; force and power are their main instruments; and security and "national interests" are their principal goals. Other Peace and Conflict Studies scholars, such as Pluralists and Contractualists, maintain that such an analysis is a strategic mistake of Realism, especially in regard to conflicts like the Israeli-Palestinian struggle. They claim that a different worldview is required to cope with these kinds of conflicts, where ordinary people and not standing armies are at the center of the confrontation.

Pluralism and Contractualism, which are relatively new paradigms in Peace and Conflict Studies, present conceptions that can be viewed as contrary to Realism. The differences are especially noticeable in the analysis of conflicts like the Israeli-Palestinian confrontation. Pluralists emphasize the impact of different social groups—such as non-governmental organizations, political parties, ethnic communities, business firms and social movements—on the development of the struggle. Contractualists emphasize the power of the people in the peace and conflict game.[14]

Realists believe that the President of the US—a power mediator with leverage—is the most suitable mediator to bring peace to the Middle East. They argue that only an intermediary with leverage could use the necessary military, political and economic power to push opposing state leaders to reach a comprehensive settlement.[15] In contrast, Pluralists and Contractualists argue that President Carter did not recognize the limits of power. According to their perspective, the Camp David Accords demonstrate the limits and the strategic mistakes of Realism.

The Second Agreement and the Limits of Shuttle Negotiation

The second agreement, "Framework for the Conclusion of a Peace Treaty between Egypt and Israel", can be viewed as the main achievement of the Camp David Accords. It created a major change in the Arab–Israeli conflict and the politics of the Middle East. However, as one might expect, the relationship between Egypt and Israel is far from being ideal.

There was no "chemistry" between Sadat and Begin, to say the least. Their different viewpoints of the desired peace process—comprehensive peace (Sadat) versus separate peace (Begin)—only aggravated the relationship between the two leaders. In principle, as specified at the beginning of this book, it is impossible to negotiate viewpoints.

Trying to negotiate viewpoints is a strategic barrier ("negotiating the impossible"). It can also create tactical barriers by provoking negative feelings, such as hostility, frustration and anger. Often enough, trying to negotiate non-negotiable issues leads to unproductive debate that has the potential to destroy any possibility to build trust and a constructive relationship.

As a desperate choice, Carter used shuttle negotiation as the main mediation instrument. He separated the parties and met with each one of them individually. He delivered the concerns, needs and demands of each party to the other in order to find the formula to bridge the gaps. Shuttle negotiation can be an effective tool to reduce the impact of negative feelings in a negotiating process. Perhaps, the intensive use of shuttle negotiation in the Camp David Accords was the only way to overcome strategic and tactical barriers. It enables two tough adversaries to reach agreements. However, there are no free lunches.

Carter did not succeed in building a good relationship between Sadat and Begin. This deficiency had a bad influence on the relationship between Egyptians and Israelis. Using shuttle negotiation as the main communication instrument did not give the leaders an opportunity to develop a cooperative relationship, which is one of the primary goals of Solution-Focused Negotiation. The relationship between Begin and Sadat remained cold and it influenced the relationships between Egyptians and Israelis. For more than forty years, there has been a cold peace between the two peoples.

The use of too much shuttle communication in a Solution-Focused Negotiation does not provide sufficient opportunities for relationship building. Building good relationships between antagonists can sometimes be no less important than the quality of the agreement. It is especially important in situations where contact between the parties is unavoidable before, during and after the negotiation (such as negotiating a divorce between devoted parents). It is recommended to use shuttle negotiation with a sense of proportion and keep in mind that Solution-Focused Negotiation is also an instrument for building good cooperative relationships.

We learned from experience that it can be useful to prepare the ground for combining different modes of communication (such as direct and shuttle) in the negotiation process. In difficult situations of conflict—where the stakes and the emotional levels are high—it is worthwhile to explain the challenges to the parties. Deepak Malhotra recommends telling the negotiators that they are going to work hard and discuss difficult, emotional and existential issues. As the process will progress, the level of bad feelings might substantially increase and they might dislike one another more and more. The parties need to be informed that this a normal process.[16] Moreover, they should look at these difficult moments as signs of progress in the negotiation.

The peace between Egypt and Israel has been quite stable. It succeeded in overcoming various challenges during the years. However, there are very few warm relationships between the peoples and mutual suspicion is still a dominant motif. The Israeli-Palestinian situation is a quite different story.

Israel and Egypt are two functioning countries with a clear border between them. Israelis live in Israel and Egyptians live in Egypt. It has been relatively easy for both sets of authorities to keep agreements and maintain a cold peace. In difficult situations of intractable conflict, like the Israeli-Palestinian situation, friction between the opposing societies is inevitable.

In the Israeli-Palestinian conflict, even an agreed upon 'two-state solution', which means political and legal divorce between the two sides, cannot create hermetic separation. Contact between Israelis and Palestinians is unavoidable in almost any aspect of social life, including geographically, economically and even emotionally. Mediators—from power intermediaries with leverage to problem-solving facilitators without any power and authority—have to take into account that 'cold peace' is probably not an option. 'Cold peace' between Israelis and Palestinians will be a strategic barrier for peacebuilding and peacekeeping.

Concluding Remarks

The Mediator's Trap—a confusion between strategic and tactical barriers—clearly shows the limitations of any human mediator. It indicates that mediators—from power intermediaries to problem-solving facilitators—who are not aware of their limitations can "fall victim" to their own biased conceptions. The question is: How can one improve the performances of mediators and help them in leading Solution-Focused Negotiations constructively, effectively and efficiently?

The challenge is to build a negotiating environment that is not entirely dependent on the good will, talent and skill of mediators and negotiators. An ideal environment, which provides a clear framework for constructive communication and an effective support system (including smart technological tools), can help in turning an ordinary person into a super mediator. At this stage, we are quite far from reaching this ideal vision, but my colleagues and I are working to approach it.

Notes

1. Peace and Conflict scholars believe that peacemaking efforts should focus on realistic goals, such as 'conflict transformation' and 'conflict management' rather than wasting time and energy in trying to reach the impossible, 'conflict resolution'. See Handelman (2023).
2. Peace has to be made, built and kept (peacemaking, peacebuilding and peacekeeping). The success of Solution-Focused Negotiation is only the first step. It does not guarantee peace and stability, especially in situations of deep-rooted conflict. A discussion about the multidimensional challenge of peace is beyond the scope of this book. For a further discussion, see Handelman (2019).
3. See Bickerton and Klausner (2007, 190).
4. Gilboa (1998).
5. A problem-solving process is often labeled 'Conflict Analysis and Resolution'. The analysis is designed to identify basic needs and fears that lead different groups to persist in a deep-rooted conflict. The resolution is agreements on mechanisms that can satisfy these basic needs and concerns. Scholars and practitioners have suggested different approaches to 'Conflict Analysis and Resolution' and named them differently. For a further discussion, see the next chapter.
6. https://knesset.gov.il/description/eng/doc/Speech_sadat_1977_eng.htm.
7. Princen (1991, 62).
8. Compare to Lax and Sebenius (1992).
9. See Bickerton and Klausner (2007, 194).
10. See Kelman (1996).
11. Bickerton and Klausner (2007, 199).
12. Bickerton and Klausner (2007, 201–202).
13. See Handelman (2019, 2021).
14. See Handelman (2016, 2021).
15. See Kriesberg (2001).
16. Malhotra (2016).

References

Bickerton, Ian J. & Klausner, Carla L. 2007. *A Concise History of the Arab-Israeli conflict*, 5th edition. NJ: Prentice Hall.

Gilboa, Eytan. 1998. Secret Diplomacy in the Television Age. *Gazette: The International Journal of Communication Studies*, 60 (3): 211–225.

Handelman, Sapir. 2016. Peacemaking Contractualism: A Peacemaking Approach to Cope with Difficult Situations of Intractable Conflict. *Global Change, Peace & Security*, 28 (1): 123–144.

Handelman, Sapir. 2019. Peace Revolution as a Three-Dimensional Process – The Israeli-Palestinian Case, in Maigul Nugmanova, Heimo Juhani Mikkola, Alexander Rozanov and Valentina Komleva (eds.) *Education, Human Rights and Peace in Sustainable Development*, London: IntechOpen. https://www.intechopen.com/chapters/70302

Handelman, Sapir. 2021. *Elements of Peacemaking Revolutions: Leaders, People and Institutions*. Newcastle upon Tyne: Cambridge Scholars Publishing.

Handelman, Sapir. 2023. Interwoven Models of Peacemaking–the Israeli-Palestinian Case and Beyond. *Diplomacy & Statecraft* 34 (4): 723–754.

Kelman, Herbert C. 1996. Negotiation as interactive problem solving. *International Negotiation: A Journal of Theory and Practice*, 1 (1): 99–123.

Kriesberg, Louis. 2001. Mediation and Transformation of the Israeli-Palestinian Conflict. *Journal of Peace Research*, 38 (3), 373–392.

Lax, David A. & Sebenius, James K. 1992. The manager as negotiator: The negotiator's dilemma: Creating and claiming value. *Dispute resolution*, 2: 49–62.

Malhotra, Deepak. 2016. *Negotiating the impossible: how to break deadlocks and resolve ugly conflicts (without money or muscle)*. Oakland, CA: Berrett-Koehler Publishers.

Princen, Tom. 1991. Camp David: Problem-solving or power politics as usual? *Journal of Peace Research*, 28 (1), 57–69.

4

Three Types of Negotiation

Bargaining, Problem-Solving and Consensus-Building

Negotiating with the Devil

Robert Mnookin presents an interesting dilemma: "Should you bargain with the Devil?".[1]

Mnookin's dilemma is limited to bargaining. Bargaining is only one form of negotiation, which is a broad concept. Negotiation means different processes to different scholars and practitioners. Accordingly, I suggest expanding Mnookin's dilemma and pose the question: Should you negotiate with the Devil?

We can identify two extreme views: Yes and No. Some claim it is almost always required to try negotiating with the Devil. Others believe you should never negotiate with the Devil. Each camp has strong arguments.

Those who reject the idea of negotiating with the Devil point out that the Devil is a cunning and unreliable beast. The Devil will find a way to deceive you. Any attempt to negotiate with the Devil signals weakness that the Devil is going to utilize, exploit and abuse for its own benefit. Those who support negotiating with the Devil remind us that the Devil is actually a human being. Like any human, the Devil has interests, needs and fears. Negotiation can be an effective tool to discover the Devil's human concerns and learn how to cope with them.[2]

The anti-negotiation camp emphasizes that human Devils often have psychopathic elements in their personalities. Negotiating with psychopaths can be very risky and dangerous. For example, the Nobel Laureate, Daniel Kahneman, pointed out that psychopaths have manipulative ability to play on our human weaknesses.[3] They can influence and operate our emotional

© The Author(s), under exclusive license to Springer Nature Switzerland AG 2024
S. Handelman, *Solution-Focused Negotiation*, Professional Practice in Governance and Public Organizations, https://doi.org/10.1007/978-3-031-52876-7_4

and irrational mind, distort our judgment and maneuver our rational mind to work in biased and disadvantageous ways. The Devil can lead you to operate against your own best interests.

The pro-negotiation camp emphasizes the power of negotiation. Negotiation—if well built, structured and designed—has the potential to successfully cope with the Devil. For example, a multidimensional approach to negotiation—which includes process, issue and timing strategies[4]—can help you overcome human weaknesses and reach negotiating agreements that can prevent the potential disaster of an aggressive clash with a powerful Devil. What should you do? How can you deal with the Devil? What are your options?

It is beyond doubt that Adolf Hitler was a human Devil. Neville Chamberlain, a former Prime Minister of the United Kingdom, had to cope with him in very difficult circumstances. Chamberlain faced our dilemma—to negotiate or not to negotiate with the Devil. He chose the negotiation path.

In 1938, Hitler was determined to gain Nazi domination in Central Europe. His next target—after incorporating Austria into Germany without a battle—was Czechoslovakia. He wanted to take the country without using force. He did not need to arouse hostile world opinion that might lead to international resistance and a full-scale war. The means to achieve such an "ambitious" goal was diplomacy, the excuse was the Sudetenland of Czechoslovakia, and the partner was Chamberlain.

The Sudetenland territory was part of former Czechoslovakia. A major part of its population—over three million people—was of German origin. Hitler demanded to annex the area to Germany. The official reason was to improve the quality of life of Sudeten Germans and prevent discrimination. History has taught us that Hitler's "real" intensions were different. However, at the time of the crisis, his genuine motivations were obscured to the rest of the world.

In retrospect, we know that Hitler was not a human rights fighter. Today, it is quite clear that his prime interest was not to improve the well-being of the Sudeten Germans of Czechoslovakia. He looked at Sudetenland as a strategic asset in his struggle to reach his political and militaristic objectives. Controlling Sudetenland would facilitate invasion to the rest of Czechoslovakia, which was another stage in the road to take over Europe.[5]

The Sudeten crisis created tension, nervousness and uncertainty in Europe. The fear was that the crisis can develop into a world war. The British leadership, at that time, believed that the United Kingdom cannot win a war against Germany.[6] Prime Minister Chamberlain decided to take the initiative. He decided to negotiate a solution to the crisis with a hungry dictator, the Devil himself.

During the crisis, Chamberlain traveled to Germany twice to meet face to face with the Fuhrer. His intensions were to get to know Hitler, understand his intensions and reach a peaceful resolution to the crisis. Perhaps Chamberlain was willing to accept Hitler's demands that were stiffening from meeting to meeting. However, these demands were unacceptable to the Czechoslovaks, the British Cabinet and the French.

In September 1938, Chamberlain arranged a four-power summit in order to prevent a war. The leaders of Britain, France, Italy and Germany met for a 2-day Solution-Focused Negotiation in Munich, Germany. They came to negotiate the future of Sudetenland (the Czech area with German origin population). Representatives of Czechoslovakia, a young country that was established in 1918, were not invited to participate in the negotiation.

Chamberlain and Hitler were very efficient in leading the negotiation. They seemed to work like a problem-solving team. They led the summit as a negotiating experiment inspired by the work of Brigadier General Henry Martyn Robert.

Brigadier General Robert wrote a manual of parliamentary procedure. The book is known as Robert's Rules of Order. In this manual, General Robert provides advice about how to run an effective multiparty meeting. One of his useful suggestions is to come prepared with decisions and agreements before the meeting starts. It seems that Chamberlain and Hitler followed General Robert's insight. They reached a solution to the crisis in their previous meetings and in private bilateral negotiation during the conference. They prepared the ground to get the support of the summit's participants.

Chamberlain had prepared the French and Czechoslovaks for the emerging solution. Hitler had prepared Benito Mussolini, the Italian dictator. During the summit, Mussolini suggested an agreement that had been secretly prepared in the German Foreign Office. Mussolini's proposal was accepted by all of the participants and became the Munich Agreement.[7]

This agreement enabled Germany to annex Sudetenland. In return, Hitler committed to allow an international committee to settle any other Garman demands regarding the rest of Czechoslovakia. Britain and Germany also signed a separate agreement that stated all future disputes would be settled by peaceful means.[8]

Chamberlain believed he had successfully prevented, at least in the short run, a bloody war that could bring disaster to Europe. Upon his return to Britain, Chamberlain announced to a cheering crowd: "My good friends, this is the second time in our history that there has come back from Germany to Downing Street peace with honor. I believe it is peace for our time".[9]

It took less than 6 months for Hitler to break the Munich Agreement. In March 1939, Hitler took over the rest of Czechoslovakia and in September 1939, Hitler invaded Poland. Two days after the German invasion of Poland, Britain—which had committed to defend Poland in case of attack—declared war on Germany.

Chamberlain's strategy to cope with the Devil came to be known as appeasement—"a policy of making unilateral concessions in the hope of avoiding conflict".[10] The conventional wisdom is that Chamberlain's appeasement is a failed negotiating strategy, or more precisely, an illusory sacrifice. Churchill, Chamberlain's successor, compared Chamberlain to "one who feeds a crocodile hoping it will eat him last".[11]

Churchill—who replaced Chamberlain as the Prime Minister of the United Kingdom during the war—refused to negotiate with Hitler (the Devil) even in the most desperate situations.[12] However, Churchill, who rejected the idea of negotiating with the Devil, claimed that appeasement is not necessarily a bad strategy. He said "Appeasement in itself may be good or bad according to the circumstances. Appeasement from weakness and fear is alike futile and fatal. Appeasement from strength is magnanimous and noble and might be the surest and perhaps the only path to world peace".[13] In a quite similar vein, the decision to negotiate with the Devil depends on the logic of the situation.

There are cases where political leaders—like Chamberlain—decided to negotiate with the Devil and there are other cases where political leaders—like Churchill—rejected the whole idea out of hand. Some of them were proved to be right and some proved to be wrong. We do not have a definite answer to the dilemma. Each decision (to negotiate or not) involves risks. This is a serious decision that has to be carefully considered.

The basic challenge is to recognize that you are dealing with the Devil and to be aware of your limitations. You will probably need to set up defensive mechanisms—such as rules, procedures and decision-making processes—to help overcome your weaknesses. Effective mechanisms will constantly remind you that you are facing the Devil.

You will need to carefully consider your moves and ask yourself difficult questions, such as: What are the possibilities to cope with the Devil? What are your terms for negotiating with the Devil? What are your negotiating strategies?

Chamberlain, the Prime Minister of the United Kingdom, decided to negotiate with the Devil. In the 1990s, the British government decided to negotiate with another type of Devil. To be more precise, the British government agreed to include political parties associated with paramilitary groups—which they considered to be diabolic beasts—in the negotiation on the future of Northern Ireland. The first case (with Hitler) ended with World War II. The second case (Northern Ireland) ended with a durable peace agreement.

The Sudetenland crisis (Britain-Germany) and the conflict in Northern Ireland are different types of conflicts. The first involves well-established states with well-organized armies. The second is a conflict where ordinary citizens, and not standing armies, are at the center of the struggle. Political leaders in each of these conflicts organized and led different negotiating settings and processes.

The decision to negotiate or not to negotiate with the Devil depends on various parameters, such as the type of conflict at stake and the negotiating strategy you intend to employ. The main purpose of this chapter is to introduce different types of negotiation—bargaining, problem-solving and consensus-building—their origins, applications and implications.

These three types of negotiation can be applied in different settings of Solution-Focused Negotiation and for different types of conflicts, from family disputes to politics. However, this chapter mainly focuses on violent political conflicts.

Bargaining, Problem-Solving and Consensus-Building

Conflict is a problem with different demands for its resolution. Solution-Focused Negotiation is an intensive attempt to reach practical and enforceable agreements that settle the conflict by peaceful means. However, negotiation is a broad concept. Negotiation involves different methods, settings and procedures for different scholars, practitioners and ordinary people.

Discussions on the meaning of negotiation often focus on three types of processes—bargaining, problem-solving and consensus-building. Each process suggests different methods, frameworks and procedures to cope with conflicts. *Bargaining* is a competitive form of negotiation, *problem-solving* is a cooperative setting for negotiation, and *consensus-building* focuses on building supportive coalitions of societal elements that can have a positive impact on efforts to resolve the conflict.

The origin of these different modes of negotiation is a historical debate in the social sciences. The debate centers around three classical paradigms—Realism, Pluralism and Contractualism. Each paradigm introduces a different worldview, emphasizes different aspects of conflicts and recommends a different peacemaking approach. Accordingly, each school of thought—Realism, Pluralism and Contractualism—advocates different modes of negotiation.

Realism, Pluralism and Contractualism are competitive paradigms. Can these competitive approaches be regarded as complementary, and how? Can it be that the three forms of negotiation—bargaining, problem-solving and consensus-building—are not necessarily in opposition? Can mediators use these different methods of negotiation simultaneously?

The Historical Debate—Realism, Pluralism and Contractualism

Realism—Negotiation as Bargaining

Thomas Schelling—the 2005 Nobel Laureate in economics—claimed that the most astonishing miracle of the twentieth century is "50 years without a nuclear war".[14] Despite the proliferation of nuclear weapons during the Cold War, there was not another nuclear attack after Hiroshima and Nagasaki during World War II. Realists believe that their sophisticated doctrine enables to explain this magic.

Realism has been the dominant paradigm in international relations. Key assumptions of classical realism are: States are the dominant actors in international politics; force and power are their main instruments; and security and "national interests" are principal goals. Realists believe that sovereign states, the key players in international politics, are self-interested social entities that are constantly engaged in power contests.[15]

Realists analyze conflicts in terms of a power struggle between competing forces. According to this view, making, building and keeping peace, order and stability (peacemaking, peacebuilding and peacekeeping) require political maneuvers associated with power politics (*realpolitik*). Implied tactics include: sanctions, threats, rewards, manipulations and determination that in the final account power has a major impact on the outcome.

Realists have emphasized that "the road to hell is paved with good intentions". In contrast, a strategy that focuses on nuclear deterrence—"I know, that you know, that I know…"—kept the two superpowers from destroying the world. The selfish interests of human beings to survive played a major part in saving the world and not morality, good intentions and altruistic motivations.

The highlight of the realist paradigm was the "peaceful" resolution of the Cuban Missile Crisis in 1962. The crisis threatened to destroy the world. There was a grave danger that the situation would deteriorate and turn into a full-scale nuclear war.

The crisis "officially" began when Americans discovered that the Soviets secretly deployed nuclear missiles on the island of Cuba. The US leadership could not tolerate the idea of nuclear missiles—that threaten the very existence of the American people—being stationed 90 miles away from Florida. Their immediate reaction was to impose a blockade on Cuba and make the necessary preparations to launch a nuclear strike within few minutes notice.

The crisis began to have a life of its own and it was not clear if the leaders had control of the situation. As Robert Kennedy, the President's brother, noted: "War is rarely intentional. The Russians don't wish to fight any more than we do. They do not want to war with us nor we with them. And yet if events continue as they have in the last several days, that struggle – which no one wishes, which will accomplish nothing – will engulf and destroy all mankind".[16]

The American and the Russian administrations succeeded in resolving the crisis within 13 days. They negotiated—directly and indirectly—solutions to the problem. They used the arsenal (strategies and tactics) of Cold War bargaining including threats, sanctions and concessions. The guiding principle of US President John Kennedy and Soviet First Secretary Nikita Khrushchev was: Nuclear war means disaster for both sides.

The opposing sides reached a settlement that addressed their interests on the basis of reciprocity: The Russians will remove the nuclear missiles from Cuba, in exchange the US government will "give assurances that there will be no invasion of Cuba" and remove American nuclear missiles from Turkey.[17]

Schelling pointed out that strategic deterrence led to the convention—"nuclear weapons, once introduced into combat, could not, or probably would not, be contained, confined, limited". This convention transformed nuclear weapons from instrument of mass destruction to a powerful means of influence and leverage in negotiations.[18]

The realist paradigm gave some satisfactory answers to major security problems during the Cold War when the two super powers competed to dictate and control world order. Moreover, the realist paradigm provided insights related to power and interests in some cases of ethnic and religious-based conflicts, such as the war in Bosnia between 1992 and 1995 following the breakup of Yugoslavia.

Richard Holbrooke, an American mediator, led an aggressive peace process to resolve the conflict in former Yugoslavia in 1995. He used American and

NATO military and economic power to bring opposing parties to the negotiating table. He used force, threats and sanctions to shape and manipulate the talks. The results of this aggressive "peace process" were the Dayton Agreement of 1995. It put an end to the Bosnian war, during which about 100,000 people lost their lives.[19] However, the success of the Dayton Accords was exceptional. The realist approach did not bring peace and stability to other intractable intrastate conflicts.

The Limits of Realism

Realists describe, relate and interpret conflict and negotiation in terms of competition. They distinguish between constructive competition—which is the key to progress—and destructive competition—which can lead to disaster. Their project is to transform destructive competition—such as violent struggle—to a constructive contest—productive bargaining by peaceful means.

Constitutional economists, such as Nobel laureate James M. Buchanan Jr., pointed out that constructive competition can emerge only in a framework of rules and institutions.[20] However, there are tragic situations of chaos, such as civil wars and interstate conflicts, without boundaries. In these situations, there are no recognized rules, and social institutions that facilitate coping with crises do not exist or do not function. How can we cope with these cases?

Unfortunately, the realist paradigm does not provide a satisfactory answer to these tragic situations.[21] Intractable conflicts can last for decades, civil wars can be fought to the finish, and weak states can collapse into vicious dictatorships and bloody chaos.[22] In these situations, core concepts of Realism—such as, balance of power, mutual deterrence and credible threats—do not provide sufficient tools for creating order and stability.

Hardcore realists often did not succeed in providing satisfactory strategies to cope with many social problems, such as protracted intrastate conflicts, bloody ethnic and religious confrontations, and widespread massacres. Indeed, Realism fell short of helping stakeholders resolve different forms of intractable disputes. One of the most notable examples is the Israeli-Palestinian conflict.

We believe that a power-based approach to peace is not always appropriate to challenges in our daily life, to say the very least. Central concepts of classical realism—terms like balance of threats, mutual deterrence and coercive bargaining—do not suit our endless efforts to peacefully cope with daily conflicts. Realist terminology and methodology do not seem appropriate to deal with confrontations—such as family disputes—where future contact between the parties is inevitable.

The limits of classical realism created an urgent necessity to approach intractable struggles from a fresh perspective. It has motivated scholars and practitioners to develop a new theoretical and practical framework to examine, analyze and cope with conflicts. However, this endeavor was not well received in academia.

The competition in the scholarly world is not about money. It is mainly about recognition, reputation and prestige. These needs are building blocks of our ego. And ego, in the sense of self-esteem, is usually non-negotiable.

Involving ego considerations in negotiation and decision-making is not recommended. It is a proven recipe for making bad decisions and reaching bad deals. Unfortunately, each one of us tends to fall in this trap and pay the price for this. For example, as a young scholar I refused a proposal offered by a well-established professor whose work I did not appreciate. The proposal was to initiate a new research and development project. According to the offer, I was to be the managing director (doing all the hard work) and the professor would be the "chief scientist". The result of my refusal was that I found myself without a job.

In the 1960s, scholars and practitioners began examining the peace and conflict game from a fresh perspective. They built a new paradigm, which they labeled Pluralism. However, international relations scholars and political scientists refused to seriously consider the new approach to conflict studies. As a result, scholars—who developed the competitive approach to classical realism—established a new independent academic discipline—'Peace and Conflict Studies'. Pluralism became the dominant paradigm in the new emerging field.

Scholars of the opposing camps—Realists and Pluralists—have been engaged in destructive competition. Most of these scholars did not join forces to examine the possibility that the competitive paradigms—Realism *versus* Pluralism—could be regarded as complementary—Realism *and* Pluralism. Unfortunately, they derided each other's ideas, underestimated each other's academic work and failed each other's students.[23]

Pluralism—Negotiation as Problem-Solving

Peace and Conflict Studies, as a distinct field of study and research, is a relatively new discipline in academia. It is difficult to determine exactly when the study began to develop as an independent discipline. However, the most active years of this academic field began in the 1960s with the pioneering work of John Burton.

The study of peace and conflicts in those days was part of international relations. And the dominant paradigm in international relations was Realism. Realism failed to provide satisfactory methods to cope with major crises—such as civil wars, ethnic struggles and intrastate conflicts—in our dynamic and ever-changing world.

John Burton was a scholar-practitioner. He was a diplomat and academician. He combined academic research with practical work in the field. He came to the conclusion that a new theoretical framework and a new practical approach are needed to cope with human problems. Burton introduced a Pluralistic approach to the study of international relations—the world society paradigm.

The world society paradigm is one form of liberal Pluralistic approach. Its key assumptions contradict cornerstones in the Realist paradigm. It points out that significant players in world politics are not limited to states. It includes different social groups that operate within and across states. These groups may include political parties, ethnic and religious communities, business firms, social movements and non-governmental organizations.

The main goals of these inter- and sub-national actors are not limited to security. They are motivated to satisfy basic physical and mental needs. These fundamental human needs include: food, shelter, security, distinct identity, dignity, social justice and independence. The most effective way to satisfy these basic needs is cooperation rather than applying national force, power and deterrence. Cooperative means include different forms of dialogue, joint research, cooperative projects and inter-organizational collaboration.

The Pluralistic paradigm has influenced the study of protracted social conflicts and their resolution. The Pluralistic approach emphasized that violent struggle is a poor strategy to achieve satisfaction of basic needs and fundamental human concerns. This fresh perspective has led to the development of a new approach to negotiation and peacemaking: Conflict Analysis and Resolution. The analysis focuses on discovering basic needs and fears that motivated opposing groups to engage in violent intractable conflicts. The resolution is agreements that address these human concerns on a basis of reciprocity.[24] Negotiation becomes a problem to be solved by the opposing parties with the help of an "impartial" mediator, a third party who is not involved, at least not directly, in the conflict.

The First Experiment—Manipulation, Negotiation and Problem-Solving

The first attempt to apply the new methodology, which Burton named "control communication", was a remarkable success. The case was a conflict that gathered momentum in Southeast Asia in the early 1960s. It involved Malaysia, Indonesia and Singapore. Burton organized a five-day workshop in London. He invited representatives of the opposing parties to meet a panel of social experts.

The official invitation was for an academic workshop—exploration and analysis of the roots and dynamic of the conflict. He did not speak about negotiation, peacemaking and conflict resolution.[25] However, we can assume that Burton's purpose went far beyond a pure "scientific" investigation of the source, structure and implications of the conflict. The workshop was a precious opportunity to employ and test the new methodology to cope with conflicts. It seems that Burton used manipulative elements to reach his goal and initiate a peacemaking process. Was it necessary?

Making an effective change in human behavior and decision-making can be very difficult. Unfortunately, it is quite common for human beings to be entrenched in biased conventions, erroneous worldviews and old habits, even when it causes them a great deal of suffering. As a desperate choice, social scientists have noted that reaching an effective change in human behavior and decision-making requires the application of manipulative elements.[26]

The trickery quality associated with manipulation enables the phenomenon to appear in almost infinite variations and under many different guises. It can be operated for indecent causes—such as Fascist propaganda—and it can be used for desirable purposes—such as negotiation, psychotherapy and education.[27] Indeed, mediators, like John Burton, often use manipulative tricks to help opposing parties settle their conflict and improve their quality of life. However, every mediator knows that the trickery elements of manipulation can create unbeneficial side effects—such as a trust crisis. Therefore, practitioners should be very careful in using this powerful tool even for the most benevolent causes.[28]

It can be very challenging to engage disputing parties in negotiation. As John Burton taught us, sometimes you need to use manipulative elements in your attitude to start a peacemaking initiative. However, once you involve disputing parties in a negotiating process, you have very limited control on the direct and indirect outcomes.

A student of mine had ongoing clashes with her husband. The most burning issue was frustrating disputes about the division of the household chores. Any attempt to peacefully discuss the issue ended with a fight. My student, who wanted to engage her husband in Online Solution-Focused Negotiation, knew that he will refuse. So, she did not have much choice but to manipulate him.

My student told her husband that she needs his help in an academic exercise. She invited him to negotiate their problem. It turned out that her husband found the negotiation useful and enjoyable. He asked his wife (my student) to continue negotiating other problems. My student—who remembered very well her previous efforts to engage him in Solution-Focused Negotiation—became quite angry. I will describe their negotiation in detail in Chap. 7.

The London workshop of Burton and his colleagues—the first attempt to use the new peacemaking methodology—was innovative. After a careful analysis of the conflict, the parties and the panelists succeeded in sketching general guidelines for settling the conflict. The workshop led to a series of unofficial talks in different forums and formats, reestablishment of diplomatic contacts between the opposing governments, official negotiations and a peace agreement in 1966.[29]

Negotiation as Problem-Solving—The Limitations

The idea to look at a conflict as a set of problems that antagonists need to jointly solve was innovative. It shifted the center of attention from the competitive aspects of negotiation to the cooperative ones. The new Pluralistic approach suggested to turn the opposing parties into a problem-solving team. I used this insight in leading different settings of Solution-Focused Negotiation. One of them is the Minds of Peace Experiment, which I have led in different forms, settings and locations.[30]

During the summer of 2012, I led another session of the Minds of Peace Experiment. Israeli and Palestinian delegations of ordinary citizens came to negotiate solutions to their conflict in the center of Tel-Aviv. The negotiation took place at one of the most famous beaches of Israel. The place was packed with people. Israelis and tourists came to enjoy the sea. We were sitting around a long table, negotiating solutions to one of the most difficult conflicts in the world.

We conducted this people-to-people negotiating assembly in such a crowded place in order to attract public attention. However, the people around us—who were dressed in bathing suits—did not really understand what we were doing. For them, we looked like strange creatures who came from another universe.

The first mission of the assembly was to reach a preliminary agreement on Trust Building Measures. The delegations had to come up with practical confidence-building steps that could be implemented immediately ("tomorrow morning"). One of the first issues that the assembly decided to discuss was the Temple Mount.

The Temple Mount is a focal point of three major monotheistic religions: Islam, Christianity and Judaism. Political activities in this holy place have the potential to instigate bloody confrontations. A tragic example is the year 2000 visit of Ariel Sharon who later became the Prime Minister of Israel.

Sharon visited the area of the Al-Aqsa Mosque. The Al-Aqsa Mosque, which is located on the Temple Mount, is a significant prayer house for Muslims. The Palestinians saw the visit as religious provocation. The result was the second Intifada (the Al-Aqsa Intifada)—a five-year outbreak of intense violence between Palestinians and Israelis.

The Palestinian delegation in our public negotiating assembly demanded to stop Israeli provocations on the Temple Mount. The Israeli delegation agreed. However, Israelis reminded Palestinians that the Temple Mount is one of the holiest places in Judaism. They explained that not every Jew who visits the Temple Mount wants to destroy the Al-Aqsa Mosque. The team (the two delegations) agreed that they need to define the meaning of "provocation". The negotiators turned into a problem-solving team. They searched for a definition that addresses the concerns of each side. The delegations agreed to examine the issue of the Temple Mount from a fresh perspective. They suggested looking at this sacred place as a symbol of peace rather than a disputed area and political tool for instigating violence. The new approach helped them to reach an agreement.

They agreed that anyone can visit the Temple Mount and the holy sites. However, each person will be permitted to pray only in places that are sacred to his or her religion. For example, Muslims could pray in mosques, Christians could pray in churches, and Jews could pray in synagogues. According to this agreement, provocation occurs when a person of a certain religion prays in a place that is sacred to a different religion. For example, if a Jew prays in a mosque or a Muslim prays in a synagogue, that will be considered a provocation.

The solution that the two delegations reached is interesting and creative. It addressed the interest of the parties to promote peace, their need to pray in dignity and security, and their fear of provocations. However, I did not see that their solution had any substantial impact on Israeli and Palestinian policymakers and it did not influence public opinion in the two societies.

In situations of political conflicts, one of the main difficulties of problem-solving engagements is to transfer insights to the operating political level and the general public. Unfortunately, it is quite rare that innovative ideas, which were discovered in problem-solving workshops, succeed in changing deep-rooted political conflicts, at least in the short run.

The London workshop of John Burton in 1966 seemed to be a huge success. However, as Ronald J. Fisher noted, it is difficult to quantify and measure the direct influence of the London workshop on the resolution of the Malaysia-Indonesian conflict. There are many other elements that played an important role in the peacemaking process.[31] Unfortunately, it is quite clear that successive attempts to resolve destructive social conflicts by the application of problem-solving interactions developed by Burton and his followers did not appear to be as successful as the first experiment.

Problem-solving workshops can be a powerful instrument to reach innovative agreements. However, not every workshop is a success. There are situations of stalemate where the parties do not know how to proceed. Indeed, Burton's 1966 attempt to recreate the success of the London workshop by using "control communication" (his peacemaking methodology) to prepare the ground for resolving the conflict in Cyprus did not succeed.

Perhaps, the biggest failures have been the various efforts to resolve the Israeli-Palestinian conflict. The infinite attempts—which include different methods of diplomacy and negotiation, various techniques of conflict resolution and involvement of several third-party mediators—did not bring peace and stability to Israelis and Palestinians. The peacemaking methods of Burton and his followers, which have been applied in the Middle East, did not succeed in resolving the Israeli-Palestinian struggle. This conflict has remained one of the most entrenched struggles in the world.

Fifty years of ongoing efforts to resolve the Israeli-Palestinian conflict is a short time relative to the duration of "classical" intractable conflicts that can last for multiple decades. However, 50 years of peacemaking efforts is a very long time for people who live in the reality of an ongoing violent struggle. We should criticize, reexamine and improve our peacemaking theories, approaches and methodologies.

The peacemaking process in Northern Ireland during the 1990s was revolutionary.[32] It is a classic example of a new approach to the peace and conflict game. It adds a new dimension to Realism (bargaining) and Pluralism (problem-solving).

Contractualism—Negotiation as Consensus-Building

Conflict in Northern Ireland

Northern Ireland is a very small place with a population of less than 2,000,000 people. However, the conflict in Northern Ireland attracted a great deal of international attention. In the 1970s, it was considered to be one of the most entrenched conflicts in the world.

The conflict in Northern Ireland is a classic case of intractable conflict. Generations were born into a reality of tension, aggression and violence. However, like almost any intractable conflict, the level of violence is not always at its peak. There are times of intense violence and there are times when the situation is more relaxed.[33]

In general, people who do not get along with each other—such as spouses who consider divorce—cannot fight "all the time". Opposing parties, in almost all dimensions of our social life—from family disputes to politics—cannot tolerate the enormous emotional, economic and social costs of ongoing high-intensity confrontations. There is a limit to the human capability to contain tensions, suffering and misery. In political intractable conflicts—which last more than a generation—the situation seems to be more acute than other types of conflicts, such as family and business disputes.

The history of most intractable conflicts seems to be structured like a tragic work of art. The different stories of these situations, often enough, include plot elements of a best seller: introduction, development, drama, tensions, hopes, disappointments and many unexpected twists along the way. The fluctuations in the intensity of violence and the dynamic of the situation enable one to divide the history of protracted social conflicts into chapters. The last chapter in the long history of the conflict in Northern Ireland is known as 'The Troubles'.

'The Troubles' began in the late 1960s. Generally speaking, it is a conflict between two communities—Unionists and Nationalists. Unionists, who are overwhelmingly Protestants, wanted Northern Ireland to remain part of the United Kingdom. Nationalists, who are overwhelmingly Catholics, wanted Northern Ireland to be part of the Irish Republic. Victimhood and fear are dominant motifs in the collective minds of both communities. Each side believed that it was the victim or, at least, feared it would become a victim in any future new social order.[34]

The Nationalists (Catholic community), who compromised about 40% of the Northern Ireland population, believed that they were a discriminated minority. However, Northern Ireland is only a small part of the Island of Ireland, most of whose inhabitants are Catholics. The Unionists (Protestant community), who compromised about 60% of the population in Northern Ireland, felt that they were a threatened minority in the larger Island of Ireland.

The Nationalists (Catholics) objected to the domination of Unionists (Protestants) and objected to continuing the union of Northern Ireland with the United Kingdom. The Unionists' (Protestants) nightmare was the unification of Northern Ireland with the Irish Republic. They believed that such a new social order would turn them into a discriminated minority.

'The Troubles'—the last chapter of the conflict in Northern Ireland—involved intense outbreaks of violence. The situation became unbearable with no end at sight. The opposing parties learned that there was no military solution to the conflict. Reaching political objectives by violent means became a non-viable option. The opposing parties also recognized that the violent struggle—which has destructive effects on all dimensions of life—was not going to be resolved spontaneously.

Desperation led leaders and political elites to initiate peacemaking processes. These initiatives did not bring peace and stability to Northern Ireland. The turning point was the all-party negotiations, which started in 1996 and culminated with the Good Friday Agreement of 1998.

The Good Friday Agreement signified the end of 'The Troubles'. This agreement was endorsed by major players in the confrontation—leaders, elites and the majority of the people. Ironically, a transformative agreement, with similar characteristics, was reached in Sunningdale—a village in Berkshire, England— in 1973, about 26 years before the Good Friday Agreement.

Both negotiated agreements focused on the institutional framework needed to transform a majoritarian rule, which was designed to ensure the hegemony of the Unionists, into a power-sharing system. However, in contrast to the Good Friday Agreement of 1998, which signified the beginning of a new peaceful era in the history of Northern Ireland, the Sunningdale Agreement collapsed into violence and despair after a few months. Why did two peacemaking initiatives that produced very similar agreements end so differently?

I believe that the difference in the essence of the two peacemaking processes is part of the answer. The lesson is: The road to reach a peace agreement is as important as the content of the agreement.

The Need for a Different Approach

From the Sunningdale Agreement of 1973 until the Good Friday Agreement of 1998, the leadership failed to bring peace and stability to Northern Ireland. The intensive use of political-elite diplomacy enabled leaders and a wide circle of political elites to negotiate solutions to the conflict and conclude different kinds of agreements. However, it was not enough to create the conditions for substantive change.

Political-elite diplomacy focuses on peacemaking interactions between official and unofficial political leaders.[35] It does not provide sufficient mechanisms to gain public trust and support for the peacemaking process. It does not provide sufficient mechanisms to enable the people to overcome classic symptoms of intractable conflicts—such as frustration, anger, chronic suspicion, existential fear, victimhood and dehumanization of the other side. Accordingly, it was easy for extremists, rejectionists and spoilers to trash the innovative peacemaking Sunningdale Accord of 1973 by intimidation, incitement and violence. A new peacemaking approach with a new type of negotiation was needed to create an effective change in this desperate situation.

The peacemaking approaches of Realism—the dominant paradigm in international relations—and Pluralism—the leading approach in Peace and Conflict Studies—focus on different settings of political-elite diplomacy. History shows that many attempts to resolve destructive conflicts by applying power-based methods (Realism) and the application of problem-solving engagements developed by John Burton and his followers (Pluralism) did not bring peace and stability. Realism and Pluralism failed to provide satisfactory methods to cope with difficult situations of intractable conflicts where ordinary people—and not standing armies—are at the center of the struggle. The peacemaking process that led to the Good Friday Agreement in Northern Ireland included strategies and tactics that Realism and Pluralism do not have. It demonstrated the urgent necessity to approach intractability from a fresh perspective.

Contractualism—a third paradigm in Peace and Conflict Studies—is designed to fill the gap of Realism and Pluralism.

Contractualism—A Third Paradigm in Peace and Conflict Studies

The pivotal players in the peace and conflict game who are missing in Realism and Pluralism are ordinary people. The Realist paradigm focuses on bargaining between state leaders. The Pluralist doctrine concentrates on problem-solving interactions between a wide circle of official and unofficial political elites. Observations show clearly that public opinion constrains leadership behavior, plays a significant role in the formation of foreign and domestic policy, and limits the influence of political elites.[36]

The Contractualism approach, a third paradigm that grows out of Realism and Pluralism, focuses upon both sets of central players in the peace and conflict game: leaders and people. Leaders are motivated by a strong desire for political power (a Realist assumption) while people, generally, strive to satisfy basic needs (a Pluralist assumption); manipulatory politics is the leaders' main instrument, while civic engagement, such as demonstrations, protests and even civil disobedience, is a tool of the people. Peacemaking becomes a consensus-building process that involves leaders, elites and people in the efforts to bring peace and stability.

Table 4.1 presents the three approaches to Peace and Conflict Studies: Realism, Pluralism and Contractualism. It emphasizes their main differences:

How can we initiate, maintain and lead a consensus-building process that involves leaders, elites and ordinary people in the struggle for change?

The consensus-building process suggests using various interactive platforms to involve various societal elements in the negotiating process. It includes, at least, two modes of interaction: political-elite diplomacy and public diplomacy. Political-elite diplomacy enables leaders to initiate a peacemaking process, negotiate solutions to the conflict and conclude agreements. Public diplomacy helps establish public support for the peacemaking process, helps people cope with crises during the struggle for change and prepares them to endorse negotiated agreements.[37]

Table 4.1 Three approaches to Peace and Conflict Studies

Paradigm	Key players	Goals	Tools	Types of negotiation
Realism	States	Security and national interests	Force, power and manipulation	Bargaining
Pluralism	Social groups	Basic human needs	Political-elite cooperation	Problem-solving
Contractualism	Leaders	Political power	Manipulatory politics	Consensus-building
	Ordinary people	Basic human needs	Civic engagement and input	

The all-party talks in Northern Ireland during the 1990s became a peacemaking institution that played a major role in producing a consensus-building effect.

Negotiating with the Devil—The All-Party Talks

The all-party talks were established to enable Northern Irish politicians to negotiate solutions to their conflict ('The Troubles'). The all-party talks, as a consensus-building instrument, needed to include legitimate representatives from across the political spectrum. It was in contrast to previous peacemaking processes which involved only a few stakeholders in the negotiations on the future of Northern Ireland. For example, the Sunningdale initiative of 1973 gave a voice only to the British and Irish Republican governments and a few moderate Northern Irish political parties.

An effective consensus-building process needed to include political parties with links to paramilitary groups. These parties had substantial influence in their communities. Their actions could have significant impact on public opinion. However, the British government regarded the paramilitary groups and their political associates as a manifestation of the Devil.

At first glance, it might have looked like the conditions were ripe for building such an ambitious multiparty negotiating process. The central players in the confrontation—including leaders of radical parties of both sides—realized that there was no military solution to the conflict.[38] Moreover, they recognized that the violent struggle—which had enormous costs—is not going to be resolved by itself. However, the inclusion of political parties with links to paramilitary groups—which the British government regarded as the Devil—in the all-party talks seems to contradict the very basic idea of a democratic consensus-building process.

One of the very basic principles of democracy is the prohibition of private armies. Naturally, the British government demanded decommissioning of paramilitary groups before any all-party negotiation begins. However, peace is made between enemies who do not trust each other and see the conflict as an existential threat. Paramilitary groups, such as the IRA, who saw the conflict as a struggle for life, refused. They insisted "there could be no disarmament until after the negotiations were completed and an agreement reached".[39]

These two ingrained positions regarding the decommissioning issue became a major obstacle for peacemaking efforts. Each side became entrenched in its position with no signs of giving up. Tragically, the ongoing violence created a momentum for change. It penetrated doubts in the position of the governments and changed the conventional wisdom.

The view that decommissioning of weapons needed to be a precondition for effective negotiation was replaced by the view that only substantial progress in the peacemaking process, with public participation and support, can lead to violence reduction. However, the parties still needed a game changer to initiate a consensus-building process that involved major players in the confrontations (leaders, elites and people).

The game changer was examining the same old problem from a different perspective. The binary question (yes or no)—"Should we include an armed Devil (political representatives associated with paramilitary groups) in negotiations that will determine the future of Northern Ireland?"—was replaced with the non-binary question—"What would be reasonable conditions for participation of key players—who can influence the results, implications and impact of the negotiations—in an effective consensus-building process?".

Senator Mitchell—the independent chairman of the peace process—sketched general conditions for the establishment of the all-party talks, a consensus-building institution. The conditions were designed to create balance between the opposing positions. They cleared the road for the participation of political parties reflecting the entire political spectrum, including parties that were associated with violence, in the negotiating process. The conditions of Senator Mitchell rested on three main principles:

1. **Principles of democratic and non-violent dialogue** (known as the Mitchell principles). Commitment to the Mitchell Principles became a precondition for participation in the peace talks.[40]
2. **A two-dimensional process.** A decommissioning process occurs in parallel with the peace talks.
3. **A program for the decommissioning process.**

The establishment of the all-party talks was an opening move in a revolutionary peacemaking journey which mobilized new groups into the legitimate political stage. They turned the Devil into a legitimate negotiating partner subject to Senator Mitchell's conditions.

The All-Party Talks—A Consensus-Building Device

The multiparty talks in Northern Ireland, known as the all-party talks, invited local political leaders and representatives of the British and Irish Republic governments to discuss, debate and negotiate solutions to the conflict. Unfortunately, the all-party talks were teetering from one crisis to another and did not show any signs of progress for quite a long time. Moreover, spoilers and radicals performed violent actions almost on a daily basis.

Most of the all-party assembly's time was spent on negotiating a framework for the discussions ('talks about talks') rather than negotiating solutions to the main problems. It took about one year and a half to negotiate ground rules, discuss decision-making procedures and reach a vague agenda for the talks. It took five months to agree on general principles for a peace pact and two weeks to conclude agreements.[41] However, the negotiations in the meeting rooms were only part of the picture.

The all-party talks created a political festival atmosphere. There were ongoing events, such as press conferences, demonstrations and scandals. Extensive media coverage of the all-party talks became a routine. All this publicity slowly began to convince the people that a peaceful negotiation could resolve long-standing political disputes. The persistence, determination and commitment of major public figures to the peace process diminished public support for the political violence path.

The all-party talks became an integral part of the daily life of the people in Northern Ireland. However, it was very difficult to progress toward resolution of the conflict. As scholars like Henry Martyn Robert and Northcote Parkinson taught us, it is very difficult to reach decisions in an assembly that includes so many political parties with different motivations and incompatible interests.[42]

An intimate forum with a very few participants was needed to reach tough decisions to complicated and existential problems. The challenge was to create an efficient decision-making mechanism, which required an intimate discussion forum, without losing public support and credibility. The solution was a two-level process: bilateral negotiations between the two governments (the UK and the Irish Republic) and multiparty negotiations in the all-party talks.

To be more specific, the decision-making procedure of the peacemaking talks included two interactive modes of communication. The governments reached decisions in "intimate" bilateral negotiations and sent drafts to the assembly. The assembly discussed the drafts and sent revisions to the governments. In practice, the all-party talks became a public diplomacy device of the two governments.

The consensus-building process was built on two kinds of coalitions—a decision-making coalition and a supportive coalition. The two governments formed a decision-making coalition—a coalition that could lead the all-party talks and bring the peacemaking initiative to conclusion. The multiparty talks created supportive coalitions—coalitions that generated public support for the talks and prepared the people to endorse solutions to major problems and disagreements.

How did it end?

Dead-Line—Last-Ditch Effort

Making decisions for human beings on critical issues is not easy. Making a choice often means paying a price, giving up options and taking a risk that the situation will become worse. This is why getting married or divorced is very difficult for some people.

The negotiations in the all-party talks centered on a new marriage contract between Unionists (Protestants) and Nationalists (Catholics). The opposing parties negotiated an arrangement for living together in peace, security, decency and stability. A new marriage contract, especially in situations of intractable conflict, requires difficult decisions from both the bride and the groom.

Unfortunately, the frustrating debate in the assembly went on and on with no light at the end of the tunnel. Ironically, it looked as if the negotiating parties knew the challenges and the risks. They understood the cost of the conflict and the benefits of peace. However, for a long time, they were not ready to make the required decisions. Senator Mitchell described the poor situation from the standpoint of a frustrated moderator: "We have been meeting for a year and a half. For hundreds and hundreds of hours I had listened to the same arguments, over and over again. Very little had been accomplished...Yet here the delegates were, furiously, debating what had or what had not been agreed to in an earlier meeting about whether we should or should not move the whole process to London and Dublin, and who said what to which newspaper".[43] The delegates used all possible tricks to avoid substantive discussion that required making real and tough decisions.

The senator's last card to "rescue" the peace process and push the delegates to move forward was to institute a hard deadline: "...without a hard deadline these people just would not decide anything...A deadline would not guarantee success, but the absence of a deadline would guarantee failure".[44] The senator's move has a lesson for our personal and social life.

I remember helping my older daughter learn how to ride a bicycle. Day after day, she was pedaling and I was running behind while holding the bike's seat. She refused biking by herself and insisted that I help her to keep balance. At a certain point, it became quite clear that she knows how to ride a bicycle and the main problem was fear.

The story of the all-party talks in Northern Ireland and the deadline of Senator Mitchell came to my mind. It made me understand that a "drastic" move is needed to "make" her start biking by herself. I announced dramatically—"Avia, if you do not start riding the bike by yourself, I am returning it to the shop tomorrow morning". She started to ride the bicycles by herself. Unfortunately, she fell after couple of minutes. I saw that she was not injured and told her that probably she was not meant to ride a bicycle and it is better to return it to the shop. This manipulative trick worked. My daughter still likes to ride bicycles and she is an excellent cyclist.

The Senator's assumption was that people who invested so much time and effort to negotiate their differences are motivated to reach agreements: "The fact that we had come this far was a testament to their perseverance. I was convinced that they were serious about dealing with the difficult issues".[45] However, they still needed a "push" to cross the bridge from conflict to peace.

The ongoing violence and the danger of escalation convinced the Senator that a time limit—a fixed deadline—is needed: "The time for discussion was over. It was now time for decision". The goal was to end the peace process before the peak of the marching season (early July). This event could be a trigger for another cycle of violence.[46]

The Final Episode

In the last phase of the negotiation, the peace process had to run like clockwork. Following the deadline of Senator Mitchell, the negotiators had two weeks to conclude a peace pact. The process to reach such an ambitious goal—a peace deal that could gain public support in two weeks—was multidimensional.

The peace process was an interactive two-level game. On the one level, the two governments became engaged in bilateral Solution-Focused Negotiation. The leaders of the UK and the Irish Republic negotiated, by themselves, solutions to the most difficult issues. On the other level, each government negotiated the outcomes of the bilateral negotiation with the relevant political party. The British government negotiated the drafts with the major Unionist party (Protestant), while the Irish government negotiated the drafts with the major Nationalist party (Catholic).

This multi-level game worked in two directions. On the one hand, negotiating the drafts with each party gave each government a good indication of which peace agreement terms the public would accept and how to formulate them in order to gain popular support. On the other hand, the same discussions helped each political party (Unionist and Nationalist) understand that peace requires painful concessions and the limits of possible compromises.

This iterative process continued until they reached a final version of the agreement. The final agreement addressed the needs and fears of the opposing sides. It included compromises that each of the political bodies and the majority of their supporters could live with.

The indirect involvement of the main political parties of Northern Ireland in the Solution-Focused Negotiation of the governments had another important aspect. It ensured that the final agreement will get the support of the majority in the all-party assembly, which had to approve the agreement. In other words, the multidimensional negotiating process created a supportive coalition of the moderate majority (the two main political parties) in the all-party assembly and marginalized the impact of radicals.[47]

On April 10, 1998, Senator Mitchel said: "I'm pleased to announce that the two Governments, and the political parties of Northern Ireland, have reached agreement".[48] The Good Friday Agreement concluded 'The Troubles', the last chapter of the violent struggle in Northern Ireland.

Concluding Remarks

Conflict is a problem with different demands for its resolution. Solution-focused negotiation is an intensive attempt to reach practical and enforceable solutions to the conflict. Negotiation is a broad concept that means different settings, procedures and processes to different scholars, practitioners and ordinary people.

This chapter introduced three types of negotiating processes: bargaining, problem-solving and consensus-building. *Bargaining* is a competitive form of negotiation. The project is to transform destructive competition—aggressive struggle—into a constructive contest—swapping demands, exchanging concessions and trading ideas that can promote a peaceful resolution to the conflict. *Problem-solving* is a cooperative form of negotiation. It is a joint search for agreements that address the interests, needs and fears of the conflicting parties "on a basis of reciprocity".[49]

Bargaining and problem-solving are ideal types. Almost any competitive process of negotiation (bargaining) contains elements of cooperation (problem-solving). And, almost any cooperative process of negotiation (problem-solving) has competitive aspects. Accordingly, bargaining and problem-solving are not necessarily in opposition.

Complex negotiations often swing between bargaining and problem-solving. The negotiation between Egyptians and Israelis over the ownership and control of the Sinai Peninsula can demonstrate this observation. It was part of the 1978 Camp David Summit which was discussed in the previous chapter.

The negotiation started with positional bargaining. Each side, Israelis and Egyptians, claimed possession of the territory. The bargaining reached a stalemate. A new approach was needed to facilitate the interaction.

A problem-solving approach—exploring the interests, needs and fears of the parties—enabled examination of the problem from a different perspective. Each side had to answer the question—"Why do you need the area?" The answers revealed different interests and needs. Israelis claimed the area because of security needs. Possession of the Sinai Peninsula provided defensible borders for Israel. Egyptians focused on sovereignty. Egyptians simply claimed that the area belongs to them from ancient times and it is part of their history, identity and self-determination.[50]

The discovery of their different interests and needs was a game changer. It enabled the stalemate to be overcome. Israelis learned that security does not necessarily require ownership of the Sinai Peninsula. There are other ways to guarantee security for Israel.

These discoveries enabled the parties to reach an agreement based on a general principle: Egypt will get the Sinai Peninsula and Israel will gain security. This general principle added bargaining elements to the problem-solving process: What are the boundaries of the area that Israel will give to Egypt?[51] What security measures—accepted by Egypt—can guarantee safety for Israel? What part of the area will be demilitarized? Etc.

The negotiation about the Sinai Peninsula demonstrated that these two forms of negotiation (bargaining *versus* problem-solving) can be regarded as complementary (bargaining *and* problem-solving). However, not every Solution-Focused Negotiation is successful. There are difficult situations where the opposing parties, with the help of a mediator, are not able to resolve the conflict by themselves. Bargaining methods and problem-solving processes do not always resolve a dispute. The negotiating assembly reaches a stalemate and the participants do not know how to progress. How can we cope with conflicts where bargaining and problem-solving processes fail to bring a settlement and stability?

Consensus-building adds another dimension to negotiating interactions. This process focuses on building coalitions of a wide circle of stakeholders who can help the opposing parties reach a viable and enforceable settlement. The assumption is that different stakeholders (such as children in a divorce proceeding) might hold the key to help the confronting parties (the parents) resolve their conflict. A key question in consensus-building is: Who should be involved in the negotiating process and how?

To conclude, a *bargaining process* is designed to cope with the problem of "How to transform destructive competition to a constructive contest?" *Problem-solving* interaction focuses on the challenge of "What are the interests, needs and fears of the opposing parties that motivate them to engage in conflict?" And a *consensus-building* process begins with the question "Who should be involved in the negotiating process and how?".

The next part of this book focuses on Solution-Focused Negotiation and its practical applications in different dimensions of our social life—from family disputes to politics. It demonstrates that each negotiation process—bargaining, problem-solving and consensus-building—requires different types of key game changers. However, it is better to look at these competitive processes as complementary.

The ability to operate different settings of Solution-Focused Negotiation can improve the performances of negotiators and mediators.

Notes

1. Mnookin (2010, 1).
2. Compare to Mnookin (2010).
3. Kahneman (2013).
4. Compare to Curran and Sebenius (2003).
5. Weinberg (1988).
6. Ripsman and Levy (2008, 150).
7. https://www.britannica.com/event/Munich-Agreement.
8. https://www.britannica.com/event/Munich-Agreement.
9. Quoted in Gladwell (2019, 45).
10. Treisman (2004, 345).
11. Quoted in Ripsman and Levy (2008, 149–150).
12. Mnookin (2010, 83–105).
13. Quoted in Ripsman and Levy (2008, 153).
14. Schelling (2005).
15. See, for example, Nye (2008, 220), Allison (1971, 2).
16. Stanton (2011, 190).
17. Stanton (2011).
18. Schelling (2005, 369): https://www.nobelprize.org/uploads/2018/06/schelling-lecture.pdf.

19. Curran et al. (2004).
20. See Buchanan (2001), Vanberg (2005).
21. I name one strategy to cope with such tragic situations-the Strong-Leader model. Thinkers-such as Machiavelli-pointed out that in these hopeless circumstances it is sometimes necessary to invite a visionary dictator to the stage of politics. The dictator's mission is to build the foundations for peace and stability by force, power and manipulation. For a further discussion, see Handelman (2023), Wantchekon (2004).
22. Compare to Huntington (2006).
23. Fisher (1997, 21).
24. Kelman (1996).
25. Fisher (1997, 21).
26. Kelman (1965), Handelman and Shoham (2009).
27. Handelman (2009).
28. Handelman and Shoham (2009).
29. Fisher (1997, 23).
30. http://mindsofpeace.org/
31. Fisher (1977).
32. Handelman (2021).
33. Azar (1978) defined protracted social conflicts as "hostile interactions between communal groups that are based in deep-seated racial, ethnic, religious and cultural hatreds, and that persist over long periods of time with sporadic outbreaks of violence.".
34. Compare to Dixon (2008, 2).
35. For a further discussion on the political-elite model, see Handelman (2023).
36. See, for example, Risse-Kappen (1991, 510).
37. See Handelman (2012, 2021).
38. Pruitt (2007, 1526–7).
39. Mitchell (1999, 29).
40. Mitchell (1999, 35–36).
41. Curran and Sebenius (2003).
42. Robert et al. (2004), Parkinson (1958).
43. Mitchell (1999, 126).
44. Ibid.
45. Ibid., 127.
46. Ibid., 143–145.
47. Compare to Curran et al. (2003).
48. Ibid., 181.
49. Kelman (1996, 99).

50. Compare with Fisher et al. (2011).
51. Following the peace agreements, a dispute over some border signs emerged between Egyptians and Israelis. The dispute focused on the subordination of a small area in Sinai Peninsula, known as Taba. It was resolved by arbitration. https://www.latimes.com/archives/la-xpm-1988-09-30-mn-3185-story.html.

References

Allison, Graham. 1971. *Essence of Decision: Explaining the Cuban Missile Crisis.* Boston: Little Brown.

Azar, Edward E., Paul Jureidini, and Ronald McLaurin. 1978. Protracted Social Conflict; Theory and Practice in the Middle East. Journal of Palestine Studies, 8 (1): 41–60.

Buchanan, James M. 2001. *Moral Science and Moral Order*, Vol. 17 of *The Collected Works of James M. Buchanan*. Indianapolis: Liberty Fund.

Curran, Daniel & Sebenius, James K. 2003. The Mediator as Coalition Builder: George Mitchell in Northern Ireland. *International Negotiation*, 8 (1): 111–147.

Curran, Daniel, James K. Sebenius, and Michael Watkins. 2004. Two Paths to Peace: Contrasting George Mitchell in Northern Ireland with Richard Holbrooke in Bosnia–Herzegovina. *Negotiation Journal* 20 (4): 513–537.

Dixon, Paul. 2008. *Northern Ireland: The politics of war and peace.* New York and Hampshire: Palgrave Macmillan.

Fisher, Roger, Ury, William L. & Patton, Bruce. 2011. *Getting to Yes: Negotiating agreement without giving in.* New York: Penguin Books.

Fisher, Ronald J. 1997. *Interactive Conflict Resolution.* New York: Syracuse University Press.

Gladwell, Malcolm. 2019. *Talking to Strangers: What We Should Know about the People We Don't Know.* New York: Little, Brown and Company.

Handelman, Sapir & Shoham, Shlomo Giora. 2009. Transference as Therapy: Psychotherapy as a Laboratory for Developing Social Theory of Change. *Divinatio* 30: 67–84.

Handelman, Sapir. 2009. *Thought Manipulation: The Use and Abuse of Psychological Trickery.* Santa Barbara, California: ABC-CLIO.

Handelman, Sapir. 2012. Two complementary settings of peace-making diplomacy: political-elite diplomacy and public diplomacy. *Diplomacy & Statecraft*, 23(1): 162–178.

Handelman, Sapir. 2021. *Elements of Peacemaking Revolutions: Leaders, People and Institutions.* Newcastle upon Tyne: Cambridge Scholars Publishing.

Handelman, Sapir. 2023. Interwoven Models of Peacemaking–the Israeli-Palestinian Case and Beyond. *Diplomacy & Statecraft* 34 (4): 723–754.

Huntington, Samuel P. 2006. *Political Order in Changing Societies*. New Haven: Yale University Press.
Kahneman, Daniel. 2013. *Thinking, fast and slow*. New York: Farrar, Straus and Giroux.
Kelman Herbert C. 1965. Manipulation of human behavior: An ethical dilemma for the social scientist. *Journal of Social Issues*, 21 (2): 31–46.
Kelman, Herbert C. 1996. Negotiation as interactive problem solving. *International Negotiation: A Journal of Theory and Practice*, 1 (1): 99–123.
Mitchell, George John.1999. *Making Peace*. New York, NY: Alfred A. Knopf.
Mnookin, Robert H. 2010. *Bargaining with the devil: When to negotiate, when to fight*. New York, Toronto and Sydney: Simon and Schuster.
Nye, Joseph S. 2008. *Understanding International Conflicts: An Introduction to Theory and History*, 7th edition. New York, NY: Pearson Longman.
Parkinson, Northcote. 1958. *Parkinson's Law*. London: John Murray.
Pruitt, Dean. 2007. Readiness theory and the Northern Ireland conflict. *American Behavioral Scientist*, 50 (11): 1520–1541.
Ripsman, Norrin M., and Jack S. Levy. 2008. Wishful thinking or buying time? The logic of British appeasement in the 1930s. *International Security*, 33 (2): 148–181.
Risse-Kappen, Thomas. 1991. Public opinion, domestic structure, and foreign policy in liberal democracies. *World politics* 43 (4): 479–512.
Robert, Henry, William Evans, Daniel Honemann, and Balch, Thomas. 2004. *Robert's rules of order, newly revised, in brief*. Cambridge, Mass: Da Capo Press.
Schelling, Thomas C. 2005. "An Astonishing Sixty Years: The Legacy of Hiroshima." Prize lecture: https://www.nobelprize.org/uploads/2018/06/schelling-lecture.pdf
Stanton, Fredrik. 2011. *Great Negotiations: Agreements that Changed the Modern World*. Yardley, PA: Westholme Publishing.
Treisman, Daniel. 2004. "Rational appeasement." *International Organization* 58 (2): 345–373.
Vanberg, Viktor J. 2005. Market and State: The Perspective of Constitutional Political Economy. *Journal of Institutional Economics*, 1 (1): 23–49.
Wantchekon, Leonard. 2004. The Paradox of "Warlord" Democracy: A Theoretical Investigation. *American Political Science Review*, 98 (1): 17–32.
Weinberg, Gerhard L. 1988. "Munich After 50 Years." *Foreign Affairs* 67 (1): 165–178.

5

Transformation
Turning Opposing Parties into a Negotiating Cooperative

The philosopher Immanuel Kant claimed that a group of rational criminals who want to function as an organized entity can form a constitution for a "decent" republic. Intelligent selfish devils, according to Kant, can agree on general rules of conduct (defined in a constitution) for their own preservation. That constitution will enable the society to function for the benefit of its members.[1] How can a group of bandits—with a certain sense of rationality—be able to form a stable republican society?

Kant, who so brilliantly described this problem, claimed it is solvable. But he did not show us how. The great philosopher left us with no solution to this puzzling riddle. I claim that Kant's intuitive vision became reality—the establishment of organized crime in America—at the Atlantic City Conference of 1929.

The Atlantic City Conference is an outstanding event in the history of the American Mafia. Representatives of criminal gangs met during May 13–16, 1929 at the President Hotel in Atlantic City. Their motivation was to stop the ongoing fighting between the various crime families.

As Immanuel Kant described the problem about 200 years ago, the crime lords, who met around the negotiating table, had conflicting interests and motivations. On the one hand, they shared a common interest—stopping the war, which was bad for business and endangered their safety. On the other hand, they had competitive interests—each one of them aspired to enlarge his territory, expand his influence and increase his profits. As Kant predicted, the crime bosses succeeded in overcoming their difficulties and came up with a constitution for a new joint organization.

It is generally accepted among historians of crime that the Solution-Focused Negotiation at the Atlantic City Conference created the foundation of a National Crime Syndicate in America. The criminals agreed on ground rules of operation, institutions for coordinating activities, and dispute resolution mechanisms. How did they do it? What are the secrets that led to such a remarkable "success"? What are the lessons that can help us create an effective framework, structure and operation of Solution-Focused Negotiation for much better causes?

Unfortunately, I do not know exactly what happened at that conference. I could not find any reliable documentation of the talks. Criminals are committed to a code of silence. However, we can assume possible scenarios. And our assumptions are based on past experience in leading complicated cases of Solution-Focused Negotiation.

In difficult cases of conflict, the first challenge is to commit the parties to the framework—rules, structure and process—of Solution-Focused Negotiation. Commitment is a powerful motivation that can help the parties critically examine their positions, consider different options and keep the process alive in times of crises. Commitment is the first step in replacing the habit of fighting with negotiation by peaceful means.

An effective way to commit the parties to Solution-Focused Negotiation is to turn them into a negotiating cooperative. What are the necessary elements for transforming opposing parties into a negotiating cooperative?

Negotiating Cooperative

Samuel Huntington, in his seminal book *Political Order in Changing Societies*, noted that three elements are necessary to turn people into a community—common interest, agreement on rules and institutions. According to this perception, common interest motivates different groups of people to form a community; agreement on general rules of conduct (a constitution) enables the community to function and guides its members to work for mutual advantage; and political institutions that reflect the other two elements (common interest and rules) are necessary for the maintenance and operation of a community. "Such institutions in turn give new meaning to the common purpose and create new linkages between the particular interests of individuals and groups".[2]

Huntington's view indicates that three elements are necessary to turn conflicting parties into a negotiating cooperative: strong desire of the opposing parties to resolve their conflict by peaceful means; agreement on constructive rules of dialogue (for example, not to demean one another); and a negotiating platform that provides procedures and organizational devices for productive talks. Are these elements enough to turn opposing parties into a negotiating cooperative that operates effectively and efficiently to resolve a conflict for the benefit of the parties?

The history of negotiations, especially in difficult situations of conflict, points out that a negotiating cooperative, often enough, does not emerge spontaneously. A visionary mediator is required to create the system and operate it. Who is an optimal visionary mediator?

A visionary mediator is a controversial term and concept. Different schools of thought suggest different visions of the optimal visionary mediator. For example, in international negotiations, realists will offer an intermediary with leverage who could use military, political and economic power to push opposing leaders to reach a settlement. Pluralists and human needs theorists will suggest a problem-solving facilitator who could help political elites of opposing parties find solutions to fundamental needs, fears and concerns that constantly fuel the conflict and make it intractable. Contractualists will vote for a consensus-building mediator who could establish effective coalitions of the pro-negotiating elements in the opposing parties against extremists and spoilers.

An ideal visionary mediator enables different strategies and tactics to be applied according to the logic of the situation. However, ideal mediators exist only in fairy tales. We saw in Chap. 3—the Mediator's Trap—that the operation of human intermediaries can be far from optimal.

How can we approach the performance of the ideal visionary mediator? How can we transform an ordinary intermediary into a super mediator? How can we construct an effective, efficient and beneficial Solution-Focused Negotiation that does not entirely depend on the good will and talent of negotiators and mediators?

Let us introduce and examine the four building blocks of a negotiating cooperative: Motivation, Rules, Platform and Leadership.

Motivation—A Strong Desire to Solve the Conflict by Peaceful Means

Motivation of the opposing parties to resolve the conflict by peaceful means is a necessary condition for effective Solution-Focused Negotiation. It takes two to tango and it requires, at least, that the two rivals start dancing around the negotiating table.

Unfortunately, it can often be very difficult to form a negotiating cooperative. It seems that the opposing parties are committed to continue fighting even when it is clearly against their best interests. They have barriers—mentally and substantially—that lead them to sabotage any conflict resolution effort. These obstacles occur in any type of conflict, from family disputes to politics.

It is quite easy to demonstrate the difficulties in situations of deep-rooted political conflicts, such as the Israeli-Palestinian confrontation, the 'Troubles' in Northern Ireland and the struggle against Apartheid in South Africa. During the long life of such conflicts, the opposing sides develop a psychological repertoire of unproductive beliefs that perpetuate the conflict. They do not trust one another. Each side believes the other side is not humane, and the conventional wisdom in the opposing sides is that the conflict is irresolvable.

Senator George Mitchell, the independent chairperson of the peace talks in Northern Ireland in the 1990s—described this tragic situation: "Later, when I became well known in Northern Ireland, I was often stopped by strangers, on the street, in the airport, in restaurants. They almost always offered words of gratitude and encouragement: 'Thank you, Senator.' 'God bless you.' 'We appreciate what you're doing.' And then, always the fear: 'But you're wasting your time. We've been killing each other for centuries and we're doomed to go on killing each other forever'".[3]

Despite the difficulties, Senator Mitchell led a quite successful revolutionary peacemaking process. The negotiations—under his leadership—succeeded in reaching the Good Friday Agreement. This agreement signified the conclusion of 'the Troubles' in Northern Ireland.

How can we identify the ripe moment for negotiation? How can we use this ripe moment to initiate a Solution-Focused Negotiation? Is it possible to create a ripe moment for negotiation?

Ripe Moment for Negotiation

William Zartman suggested a theory of "Ripeness for Negotiation". According to Zartman, two necessary conditions are required to motivate conflicting parties to meet around the negotiating table:

- The opposing parties are in a costly stalemate that could lead to a major catastrophe.
- The opposing sides identify possibilities to reach a negotiated solution that can improve their situation.[4]

The history of peace and conflict indicates that Zartman's analysis sketches only a partial picture of a complex reality.

Zartman's first condition, indicates that the desire to break a situation of "a mutually hurting stalemate" is incentive to negotiation. Both sides understand that it is impossible to defeat the rival and the conflict will not vanish or be resolved by itself. They come to the conclusion that it is impossible to "win" the conflict by force. And, the status quo of ongoing struggle becomes too costly. For example, the people in Apartheid South Africa understood that political change was inevitable. The March 17, 1992 referendum—which was limited to *white* South African voters—showed clearly that the majority of the white voters supported negotiated reforms that can put an end to the Apartheid system. It was also clear to the *non-white* camp that the liberation movement would not be able to overthrow the Apartheid regime by force.

During the "Troubles" in Northern Ireland, the parties understood that there is no military solution to the conflict. The British government and unionists (Protestants) understood that it will be impossible to defeat paramilitary groups, such as the IRA, by military force, while nationalists (Catholics) realized that achieving their political objectives, such as driving out the British army from Northern Ireland, cannot be achieved by violence.

"Mutually hurting stalemate" can be a strong incentive for making serious attempts to resolve the conflict by peaceful means. However, it is not enough to bring the parties to the negotiating table. There are powerful barriers to conflict resolution that push the parties away from negotiation. I suggested labeling these conflicting motivations the 'Paradox of Stalemate'.

The 'Paradox of Stalemate' describes the ambivalence of the conflicting parties. On the one hand, it becomes clear to them that the conflict cannot be resolved by force and the intolerable situation can come to an end only around the negotiating table. On the other hand, the ongoing aggressive confrontation contributes to the entrenched belief of each side that the other is not a partner for negotiation and peace ("They are not human beings").

History shows that a new visionary leadership is needed to resolve the paradox. In many cases of intractable conflict—such as the 'Troubles' in Northern Ireland and the struggle against Apartheid in South Africa—visionary leaders emerged on the political stage and initiated revolutionary peacemaking processes.

In contrast to Zartman's second condition (optimism about negotiation results), it is hard to believe that opposing parties have positive expectations from the negotiation. Optimism might be a motivating incentive, a moral obligation or a necessary element in the relationship, but it is rare merchandise in situations of deep-rooted political conflicts. It is more realistic to believe that the opposing parties are willing to try to negotiate solutions to their conflict as a desperate choice. But this is not the whole story.

The parties still need glimmers of hope to commit themselves to a negotiating process. Senator Mitchell used various manipulative tricks to inspire hope among the negotiators and the general public. For example, he stated that the political violence in the streets is a sign that the peace process is moving forward and the negotiation is progressing. These tactics were necessary to keep the process alive in difficult situations of crisis where the talks were about to collapse.

Zartman's project is to identify conditions of ripeness for negotiation in situations of deep-rooted conflicts. The challenge in this book is broader. We look for ways to motivate conflicting parties to meet around the negotiating table. Zartman's two conditions for ripeness—the status quo of ongoing conflict becomes intolerable and optimism from negotiation—are not enough. Moreover, we do not want the intensity of the conflict to escalate toward a catastrophe.

How do we motivate entrenched rivals to negotiate solutions to their conflict in a good faith?

Different Perspectives, Creating Value and Back-Door Mediation

Competitive rivals in one dimension can find incentives for cooperation in a different dimension. For example, entrenched enemies can join forces to fight a common adversary. Rival ethnic groups in South Africa—who hated each other—united to fight the Apartheid system. In Solution-Focused Negotiation, the joint enemy should be a negotiation problem.

Conflicts have implications in multiple dimensions. For example, disputes over the division of property between divorced parties can influence the well-being of their children; inheritance conflicts might impact family cohesion; and unrestrained competition between political entities has the potential to endanger the stability of a region.

Unfortunately, conflicting parties tend to see a distorted vision—a one-dimensional picture of the conflict and its implications. They tend to behave as if they are fighting in a battlefield. Examining the conflict from different perspectives might give them a sense of proportion.

Enlarging the picture—by examining the conflict from different angles—can help identify powerful incentives for adversaries to engage in Solution-Focused Negotiation. It can show the parties that both of them can benefit from a negotiated agreement. In professional terms, broadening the picture opens possibilities for "creating value". How can we do this?

Discovering new vistas can be challenging, especially in situations of entrenched conflict. The mediator needs to be attentive, creative and knowledgeable. On the one hand, the mediator has to be familiar with the parties and their preferences, viewpoints and motivations. On the other hand, the mediator has to examine the situation as an expert who is mentally detached from the conflict. How can we find such a super mediator?

Back-door mediation, which engages conflicting parties in Online Solution-Focused Negotiation, could be useful to cope with the problem. Back-door mediation involves an acting mediator and a secret advisor. The acting mediator is an 'involved mediator', an intermediary who knows the parties (such as a family member, a friend or a colleague). A secret advisor is a professional mediator who observes the negotiation and provides suggestions to the acting mediator.

This technique enables us to combine the practical knowledge of the involved mediator (the acting mediator) with the skills of a professional intermediary (the secret advisor). My colleagues, students and I used Back-door mediation to involve conflicting parties in Online Solution-Focused Negotiation. We have developed the tool and adjusted it for different types of conflicts.

In many of our cases and experiments, the acting mediator—who knows the parties and speaks the same cultural language—incentivized them to negotiate their differences in good faith (creating value). The secret advisor used his or her professional skills, experience and knowledge to identify key game changers, which were necessary to begin, maintain and conclude the process. In short, Back-door mediation helped the acting mediator become a super intermediary.

The acting mediator is familiar with the parties and knows their preferences, sensitivities, vulnerabilities and ambitions. It is much easier for the acting mediator to add other dimensions to the negotiating problem. These additional dimensions can create strong incentives to end the conflict by peaceful means. In the terminology of negotiation scholars, the acting mediator can create value. Creating value—adding incentives to end the conflict by peaceful means—can be very important for any kind of negotiation from family disputes to politics.

For example, a sister told her brothers that their father will not rest in peace until they solve their inheritance conflict. A friend of a married couple explained to each of them that solving their dispute over their place of residence is necessary for the well-being of their children. "Someone" close to both the Israeli defendant Prime Minister and the Attorney General can tell them that reaching a negotiated plea bargain can benefit the Israeli people.

Creating value—generating incentives to negotiate in good faith—does not guarantee success. The parties still need to find negotiated solutions to their conflict. Often enough, it is not easy.

In our examples, the siblings need to reach a negotiated arrangement for the division of their inheritance that—according to their beliefs—enables their late father to rest in peace. The married couple needs to choose a place of residence that can benefit their children. The defendant Prime Minister and the Attorney General still need to reach a negotiated plea bargain that meets their interests and the interests of the Israeli public.

The first two examples—the brothers and the married couple—are real-life cases. I was involved in these negotiations and I describe them in this book. The third example relates to the ongoing trial of the Israeli Prime Minister—Benjamin Netanyahu. I do not have any connection to the trial of the Prime Minister. I briefly presented a possible scenario according to the framework of the discussion here.

To conclude, motivation to solve the conflict by peaceful means is a necessary condition to engage disputing parties in Solution-Focused Negotiation. It is the first building block in turning conflicting parties into a negotiating cooperative. If one of the parties is not motivated to negotiate, then negotiation is usually not a viable option.

Motivation to negotiate is a function of several variables, including: Interests—a shared interest to resolve the conflict by peaceful means; Timing—a window of opportunity to initiate productive negotiation; and Expectations—fear of conflict escalation and hope for a successful negotiating process.

Examining the conflict from different perspectives can generate powerful incentives to negotiate (creating value). An involved mediator—who knows the parties quite well—can be very effective in generating incentives to negotiate (creating value). However, engagement and commitment to negotiate in good faith does not guarantee success. A professional mediator—who has knowledge and expertise—can help identify key game changers that are needed to cope with negotiating problems, to overcome crises and to conclude agreements.

Back-door mediation requires an involved mediator (the acting intermediary) and a professional mediator (the secret advisor) in Solution-Focused Negotiation. This combination can improve the process and outcome of the interaction.

Rules—Commitment to Constructive Rules of Negotiation

Negotiation starts with competition. Opposing parties demand different solutions to a shared problem—business partners push their company in opposite directions; a married couple fight over the custody of their children; and Israelis and Palestinians have different claims over ownership of the holy places in Jerusalem.

Competition can be constructive or destructive. Constructive competition—such as innovation contests in a free market system—can improve the quality of life. Destructive competition—such as intractable conflict and civil war—can lead to disaster. Free market economists and constitutional economists argue that constructive competition can emerge only in a framework of general rules (a constitution) and institutions.[5] In our context, the question is: What are the general rules that transform destructive competition—ongoing fighting and confrontation—to a constructive contest—bargaining by peaceful means?

Scholars of Peace and Conflict Studies argue that bargaining is only one form of negotiation. Negotiation is a broad concept that includes other forms of interaction, such as problem-solving (cooperation) and consensus-building (constructing coalitions). The more inclusive question is: What general rules are necessary for transforming parties engaged in a conflict into a joint negotiation cooperative?

Two General Ground Rules

Our experiments indicate that there are two general ground rules for effective Solution-Focused Negotiation:

1. To show respect and not demean one another.
2. Avoid historical debate upon the origin of the conflict and the causes of past evils.

Both of these rules are designed to facilitate thinking from a different direction and dimension.

Two Interactive Systems of Thinking and Operation

The best minds of humanity have been struggling with this highly controversial question: What is the very nature of human beings?

The discussion emerges between two extremes: On one side, we can place scientists and philosophers who believe that human beings are rational creators. On the other side, we can locate scholars and practitioners who claim that human beings are irrational animals.

No doubt each of us has rational and irrational motivations and incentives for action. Nobel Laureate Daniel Kahneman suggested that those patterns belong to two interactive systems: the irrational mind (system 1) and the rational mind (system 2).[6] Kahneman suggests a useful, schematic and metaphorical division of our mind. His suggestion enables us to discuss the dispute over the nature of human beings in a pragmatic manner: Which is the dominant system: the irrational (system 1) or rational (system 2)? Can it be that irrational mind (system 1) controls and operates rational mind (system 2)? Or, is rational mind (system 2) able to restrain, control and manipulate irrational mind (system 1)?

The different answers have led negotiation scholars and practitioners to suggest different modes of operation. Some suggest approaching rational system 2 and others propose approaching irrational system 1. Both camps have argued that their methods of operation can lead negotiation to a successful conclusion.

Roger Fisher and William Ury, in their best-selling book *Getting to Yes*, and Harvard psychologist Herbert Kelman suggest approaching rational system 2 in order to turn opposing parties into a problem-solving team. In contrast, the former FBI negotiator, Chris Voss, in his seminal book *Never Split the Difference*, proposed approaching irrational system 1 of negotiators by using 'tactical empathy'. 'Tactical empathy' is designed to establish rapport with negotiating partners in order to maneuver their thoughts and modes of operation.

The philosophers Karl Popper and Joseph Agassi would probably claim that it is impossible to conclude if human beings are 'rational creators' or 'irrational animals' We are complicated entities. The human mind is probably built of different elements. Our decisions, attitudes and actions are the result of rational considerations and calculations and irrational motivations and incentives. Mediators are required to operate according to the logic of the situation and use their knowledge and expertise. This is our approach here and in the Negoflict project, which provides a digital platform for Solution-Focused Negotiation.

Each ground rule of the negotiating game is designed to approach a different system. The first rule (show respect and avoid insults) is designed to approach system 1 (the irrational mind). The second rule (avoid historical debates) is designed to approach system 2 (the rational mind).

First Rule—Do Not Demean One Another and Do Show Respect

In situations of ongoing conflicts—such as, clashes between family members over the same old topics—the parties tend to develop bad communication habits. They constantly use provocations, insults and even intimidations. They are wasting time and energy by fighting instead of making joint efforts to come up with practical solutions to difficult problems. Impulsive reactions overcome rational and practical thinking.

In these tragic situations, it seems to be much easier to surrender to the urge and pressure of the irrational and impulsive mind (system 1) than to invest energy and effort in operating the rational mind (system 2). The parties and their social circle pay a heavy price for the ongoing clashes and their destructive behavior. They need help and guidance.

Friedrich Hayek, the Nobel Laureate in Economic Sciences in 1974, taught us that "rules are tools". Rules help us overcome bad habits and guide us to operate for our personal and social benefit. The first part of the first rule—"do not demean one another"—is the beginning in controlling our automatic reactions (system 1). It maneuvers the parties to start seriously listening to one another, which is the first step in discovering the interests, needs, and fears of the other.

A student of mine complained about ongoing clashes with her teenage daughter. Their "favorite" topic of fighting was—the household chores. The mother complained that her daughter never helps with the household work and their home is always a mess.

The mother reported that any attempt to discuss the topic with her daughter turned into a battle of shouting. They simply refused to listen to one another. Another student of mine engaged the mother and her daughter in Online Solution-Focused Negotiation. The parties agreed to commit to the rules of the negotiating game.

The rules of the game provided a framework for constructive communication. They had to avoid using the same old patterns of accusations and historical debates (such as—who started the fight and who did what to whom). They had to focus on their needs and interests and listen to each other. As the discussion progressed, it turned out that the refusal of the daughter to help in the household chores was an act of protest. It was her way (or more precisely her distorted way) to cry for her mother's attention. She felt that her mother was not there for her.

The mother, who is a single parent, was extremely busy. She worked a full-time job, studied for courses at a college and was always exhausted. The daughter felt they hardly spent any quality or quantity time together. The daughter was embittered that her mother never has time to spend with her and when she has time, she is always tired.

This was a major discovery, at least for the mother and the mediator. It illuminated the interaction and the 'negotiating problem' in a completely different light. The question was: What to do with such a groundbreaking discovery?

The first part of the first rule of the negotiating game—"not to demean one another"—is designed to enable constructive communication. It helps the negotiators express their interests and needs and listen to each other. The second part of the first rule—"to show respect to each other"—is designed to help the parties build empathy. Research shows that empathy creates positive emotions (system 1) that can activate rational thinking (system 2).

Chris Voss—a former FBI hostage negotiator—demonstrated the motivating power of empathy. As a negotiator he used tactical empathy to stimulate positive feelings (system 1) that can activate the rational mind (system 2) to operate in the "desirable" direction (release the hostage). To put it differently, he used empathy as an effective tool to maneuver the kidnaper to come up with possible solutions to his (Voss's) problem.

Chris Voss's purpose is to "win" the negotiation. He uses a sophisticated manipulative method—tactical empathy—to lead the other party to do whatever he wants (release the hostage). The purpose of Solution-Focused Negotiation in this book is different.

The structure and operation of Solution-Focused Negotiation is designed to help negotiating parties reach agreements of mutual advantage. Building empathy between the parties enables exploration of solutions that can benefit both sides. It enables one to find solutions that address the concerns, interests and needs of the parties.

In our case, the mother and her teenage daughter began to explore solutions that addressed *the daughter's need* for her mother's attention and *the mother's need* that her daughter will share responsibility in keeping the house clean and tidy. They reached an agreement. The agreement created balance between the different needs of the parties and took into account the constraints of reality. For example, the mother still has to work in order to bring food to the table.

The first rule of the negotiating game—"do not demean one another and do show respect"—is a good starting point. It enables the parties to seriously listen to one another, explore the interests, needs and fears of each side and develop mutual empathy. However, it is certainly not enough to bring negotiations—especially in difficult situations of conflict—to a successful conclusion.

Second Rule—Avoid Historical Debate about the Origin of the Conflict and Past Evils

As an old saying goes "You cannot start the next chapter of your life if you keep re-reading the last one". In conflicting situations, each opposing party tends to rewrite the past. In Kahneman's terminology, the emotional mind (system 1) is controlling the rational mind (system 2) in an unproductive manner.

Most conflicts start with a real substantial problem (not everything is psychology): "How to convince our daughter to go to school?", "How to cope with an economic crisis?" and "How to build a decent liberal society in Northern Ireland, South Africa and Israel?".

These are serious difficult problems. We need to invest much energy in operating our rational thinking (system 2) to come up with various solutions to such challenging problems. It seems to be much easier to surrender to our impulsive negative feelings (system 1).

Instead of coping with real problems—which probably will not vanish or get resolved by themselves—each party constructs a good story of the history of the conflict. They tend to fall in love with their construction and present it as the ultimate truth. The tragic result is a blame game that can lead to the collapse of any problem-solving interaction. This unproductive communication is quite common in situations of ongoing tensions and distresses in almost all walks of life from family disputes to politics.

It is quite easy to imagine a tragic scenario where a young teenage girl refuses to go to school. Her parents are confused and do not know how to handle the situation. They are frustrated.

In theory, they can calm down, explore different alternative solutions to cope with this unpleasant and worrying situation. They can even decide to ask for professional help. Unfortunately, their first impulsive reaction (operating by system 1) is to start with historical accusations that escalate into an unproductive and destructive blame game—"You spoiled her too much", "I told you, a long time ago, that she needs therapy", "This is a direct result of the only thing you care about—your career" and "She inherited all her bad qualities from you". These accusations—whether they are sophisticated or primitive—will not bring the young girl back to school.

The second rule—Avoid historical debate about the origin of the conflict—is designed to keep the parties from sliding into an unproductive blame game. It tends to "empower" the rational system 2 to restrain the irrational and impulsive system 1. Solution-Focused Negotiation is not a courtroom or a laboratory for the study of history.

Historical exploration about the source of the conflict is not beneficial for the negotiation, to say the least. It can quite easily lead to clashes between different and opposing viewpoints which can turn the negotiation into a frustrating historical debate. This is a proven recipe for the collapse of the negotiation. Intractable conflicts, such as the endless Israeli-Palestinian struggle, demonstrate this complication.

The 1948 war between Israel and various Arab states, which started after the Israeli Declaration of Independence, created about 750,000 Arab refugees. The opposing sides developed different narratives to this tragic disaster. Israelis claim that Arab armies attacked the new state of Israel. Moreover, according to this narrative, the Arab leaders told the Arab inhabitants of the area (Palestinians) to evacuate their homes in order to facilitate the military effort to dismantle the Jewish state. Palestinians tell a completely different story. They claim that Israelis simply deported the Arab inhabitants from their homes by force and intimidation.

Each of these narratives is probably a one-sided construction of a complex reality. Nevertheless, generations of Israelis and Palestinians were educated to believe that their constructed narrative is the ultimate truth. Any attempt to find out the truth around the negotiation table will probably turn the interaction into an endless frustrating debate between opposing viewpoints and beliefs.

It is quite clear to everyone involved in the conflict that the problem of the Palestinian refugees is one of the core issues of the confrontation. It is common knowledge that there will not be a viable solution to the conflict without addressing this problem. A practical solution that takes into account the interests of both sides is needed, not a frustrating historical debate.

Scholars and practitioners have suggested practical solutions to this difficult problem. Moreover, people-to-people initiatives—such as the Geneva Initiative[7] and the Minds of Peace Experiment[8]—showed that the problem is negotiable and solvable. Unofficial political elites and ordinary citizens of both sides demonstrated, again and again, that it is possible to find a negotiated practical solution to this problem.

A good chess player knows that he or she is not alone in the game. A good negotiator has to take into account that the other side has a different perspective of the situation. The second rule—avoid historical debate—helps remind each party that the time has come to move forward and look for practical solutions.

Historical Justice Versus Practical Justice

Opposing parties hold different views of the conflict. Turning the negotiation into a joint search for the ultimate true story of the conflict is destined to create a clash between viewpoints. Any attempt to turn the negotiation into a historical court of justice is not an effective way to find practical solutions to a conflict. It has the potential to bring the negotiation to a dead-end. A different perspective of justice is required for those who care about fairness—practical justice.

Every decent mediator knows that life is not fair and social life is not symmetrical. People are *not* equal: there are rich people and poor people; there are strong people and weak people; there are educated people and less educated people; there are kind people and less kind people.

Naturally, conflicts are not symmetrical. Different kinds of people are engaged in different kinds of conflicts. The diversity of human beings makes the discussion on justice—in the context of negotiation and conflict resolution—challenging. A search for historical justice—that will be accepted by the negotiating parties—seems to be an impossible mission. The psychologist Herbert Kelman suggested adding the differences between human beings to the justice equation. I suggest giving the label 'Practical Justice' to the perspective of justice introduced by Kelman.

Kelman looks at negotiation as a problem-solving interaction—a joint attempt to reach "an agreement that addresses the fundamental needs and fears of both parties on a basis of reciprocity".[9] According to Kelman, by addressing the main concerns of the parties, the negotiating interaction is providing a certain level of justice for them. In Solution-Focused Negotiation, it is better to look for partial and imperfect justice (practical justice) than to try to reach an unrealistic goal, such as historical justice.

The second rule of Solution-Focused Negotiation—"avoid historical debate"—is not a request that the parties forget history. The opposing parties cannot forget their history—or more precisely their constructed history of the conflict—which is sometimes part of their identity. The main purpose of the second rule is to focus their attention and efforts on a joint search for practical solutions to their conflict.

Negotiating Platform

A negotiating platform provides communication channels to activate, operate, support and lead the negotiating cooperative. It enables the opposing parties to engage in a joint search for practical and enforceable solutions to their conflict. Negotiating platforms are the operational manifestation of the common desire to resolve the conflict by peaceful means and the commitment of the parties to the rules of the negotiating game. Negotiating platforms provide interactive channels of communication. The channels can be face-to-face, online or a combination of these.

In a conflict between two parties, the basic requirement to be satisfied by a negotiating platform is to provide direct and indirect negotiating channels. Direct negotiation enables the parties to negotiate their differences with each other under the leadership of a mediator. Indirect negotiation is often called 'shuttle negotiation'.

In shuttle negotiation, there is no direct contact between the negotiators. The mediator meets with each party separately and delivers messages between them. Shuttle negotiation can be very useful before the actual negotiation begins and in times of difficulties and crises during the negotiation.

In the introductory stage of Solution-Focused Negotiation, the mediator meets separately with each party. This meeting enables the mediator to better understand the topic of the conflict and prepare each party—intellectually and emotionally—for the talks. During the meeting, the mediator explains the process to each party and asks them to think about possible solutions. The mediator can even help them to develop strategies to cope with the situation.

A productive meeting enables the mediator to begin maneuvering the mindset of each side. It helps the negotiators concentrate on a constructive search for possible solutions to the conflict instead of the "usual" destructive patterns of fighting (blame game, slanders and intimidations). In the terminology of the psychologists Tversky and Kahneman, the first introductory meeting is intended to anchor in the minds of the parties—"the conflict can be resolved".

This strategy is employed in Brief Solution-Focused Therapy, which shares similarities with Solution-Focused Negotiation. Psychologists claim that the therapy starts with the first phone call. When the client calls to ask for help, the therapist gives him or her "homework" during this first conversation. The therapist asks the client to think about practical solutions to his or her misery and come prepared to the session. In my classes, students shared their conflicts and together we explored strategies to handle their distress. We turned the class into a conflict resolution laboratory.

One student presented his or her conflict and the others provided recommendations for coping with the situation. This brainstorming enabled the students to approach the conflict from different perspectives. It works in two directions. On the one hand, it helped the student, who was involved in the conflict, plan a strategy for the actual Solution-Focused Negotiation. On the other hand, it trained that student to listen constructively, remain flexible and be prepared for different and unexpected scenarios during the real negotiating interaction.

Solution-Focused Negotiation is a deal-making device and relationship-building instrument. A basic negotiating platform provides channels for direct and indirect interaction. It is recommended to use shuttle negotiation (indirect negotiation) with a sense of proportion. True, in difficult cases of negotiation, the use of shuttle negotiation is unavoidable. However, too much use of shuttle negotiation does not leave much time for building relationships. It is important to bring the parties together, especially in situations where complete detachment is impossible and future contact is inevitable.

Human Limitations and Support Systems

Conflicts can be complex. They have a major impact on different areas and dimensions of our social life. For example, intractable conflict—a conflict that lasts more than a generation—is a classic example of a 'complex phenomenon'. Intractable conflicts, such as the Israeli-Palestinian situation, have components in almost every imagined and unimagined dimension, including psychology, sociology, anthropology and economics.

How can a human mediator cope with such a complicated phenomenon? How can we improve the performance of human mediators? How can we build an effective platform for Solution-Focused Negotiation that is not entirely dependent on the goodwill, talent and motivation of a human mediator?

The first thing that comes to mind, when dealing with such questions, is computer technology (such as Artificial Intelligence). My colleagues and I believe that, at this stage, computers cannot replace human mediators, at least in the more difficult cases of conflict. There has to be a third-party human intermediary in the negotiation loop. However, computer technology and other kinds of support can improve the performance of human mediators. Moreover, an effective support system can turn an ordinary human intermediary into a super mediator. Let me share some practical ideas.

Back-Door Mediation

Back-door mediation combines the operations of acting mediator and secret advisor. The acting mediator leads the negotiation, while the secret advisor provides suggestions and insights. In my classes, the acting mediator was a student who is involved in the conflict or knows the parties (for example, a family member, a friend or a colleague), while the secret advisor was a professional mediator.

We have led dozens of Online Solution-Focused Negotiation by using text messaging platforms. The negotiated cases were real and not simulations. Some of the cases were difficult and complicated, such as a bitter inheritance conflict that lasted more than 20 years. Others were common distrustful situations, such as a conflict between a married couple on the appropriate division of household chores. We provided an accessible opportunity for students and their associates to cope with conflicts in their personal and professional lives. The service was free of charge.

In most cases, the use of Back-door mediation was very effective. The two mediators complemented each other. In many cases, the 'acting mediator' created motivation to negotiate, led the negotiation and enforced the rules of the game, while the 'secret advisor' (the professional mediator) identified key game changers.

As stated previously, the acting mediator (the involved intermediary), is usually familiar with the conflict, speaks the language of the parties and has the ability to influence their attitude and behavior. The secret advisor (the professional mediator) examines the conflict from a distance (he or she is not emotionally involved), adds another angle of vision to the analysis and brings his or her experience to the negotiating table.

Back-door mediation can be an effective tool to improve the effectiveness of Solution-Focused Negotiation.

Artificial Intelligence (AI) Tools

Let me briefly introduce some AI tools that can have a positive impact on the course, operation and the results of Online Solution-Focused Negotiation.

Text Analysis—The most basic application can help enforce the first rule of the negotiation—"not to demean one another". An online platform can detect inappropriate language, such as intimidations and provocations. The computer can send alerts to the mediator and negotiators.

The more sophisticated AI (artificial intelligence) tools can be adjusted and developed to enable successful conclusion of Solution-Focused Negotiation. For example, they could give an indication whether the parties are getting close to agreement or the opposite; they could identify patterns that appeared in other cases and send recommendations; and they might have the ability to analyze the interests, motivations and fears of negotiators.

This project is beyond the scope of this book. The Negoflict initiative—a digital platform for Solution-Focused Negotiation—will incorporate AI tools in the system. I will provide more details about this challenging project in the next chapters.

Sentiment Analysis—Sophisticated AI tools can help identify negative and positive emotions in the text. In case of negative emotions, the computer can send an alert to the negotiators and the mediator. The mediator can decide how to deal with this information. He or she can decide to change the online platform to shuttle mode (indirect negotiation), try to chill the interaction or ignore the warning alert. In case of positive emotions, the mediator can decide to continue leading the negotiation in the same direction, float a trial balloon or use the momentum to propose an innovative idea that can lead to a turning point in the interaction. Of course, to make a smart decision, the mediator will need much more information.

Smart Database—Often enough, the participants in Solution-Focused Negotiation reach a stalemate. The mediator and the negotiating parties are stuck and do not know how to progress. They need an idea that can help them advance the negotiation.

My colleagues and I are building a database that includes classic barriers for conflict resolution and insights to overcome the obstacles. This is a topic for the next book. The last chapter in this volume, which focuses on key game changers, serves an introduction to this topic.

Visionary Mediator

History shows that a main part of a social conflict starts or centers around "real problems". The phenomenon of "real substantial problems" leading to entrenched conflicts emerges in almost all dimensions of the social life—from family disputes to international politics: How to divide the house work between family members? Who is going to be the President of the union? How to allocate social resources in the most efficient and effective way? And, how to prevent the proliferation of nuclear weapons?

We can assume that in an ideal world of rational human beings, "real problems" could be resolved around the negotiation table. In the terminology of Fisher and Ury—the authors of *Getting to Yes*—in an ideal world, in principle, it is possible to find an objective criterion that can help the negotiators reach practical and enforceable solutions to "real problems".

However, we do not live in an ideal world of rational human beings. Conflicting parties, as human beings, have emotional and intellectual barriers. These barriers can motivate them to behave against their own best interests and block any possibility of reaching agreements of mutual benefit. This devastating phenomenon occurs again and again, even when the continuation of the conflict creates a great deal of suffering and misery to the parties and their social environment.

In these tragic situations, the conflicting parties need assistance. The three basic building blocks that constitute a negotiation cooperative—**Motivation** to resolve the conflict by peaceful means, commitment to **Rules** of constructive talks and an efficient negotiating **Platform**—are sometimes not enough to resolve the conflict. As the following example demonstrates, the parties need a "visionary mediator"—the fourth element.

A sister and her brother divided the property that they inherited from their late parents, except for one asset. They could not come to an agreement about the ownership of the family's car. The monetary value of the car was almost insignificant compared to the monetary value of the rest of the property.

The older brother claimed the car for himself. He took care of his sick parents while his sister completed her graduate studies. He used his parents' car while they were sick and he claimed that he should own it. His sister, who received her mom's jewelry, objected. She demanded to split the value of the car equally. The dispute aggravated the relationship and they hardly spoke to each other. They asked the help of a mediator that they both knew and trusted.

The sophisticated mediator asked the brother if he is willing to lend his sister an amount of money that is triple than the value of the car. The brother answered that he is willing to give the money as a gift if his sister really needs it. The mediator showed him the paradox in his attitude toward her sister: On the one hand, he is not willing to split the value of the car with his sister. On the other hand, he is willing to give her triple than its value.

The mediator explained to the brother that the insignificant monetary value of the car is not the issue. The brother was 5 years old when his sister was born. Since then the idea "she took my parents from me" played a significant role in his attitude toward her. It is the inner five years old child that still fights for his parents' full attention that motivates his irrational behavior.

In a similar vein, the mediator explained to the sister the source of her inflexibility. She was always the little sister who had to struggle for her status in the family. She wanted to be heard and not to be treated as the "little girl". She developed uncompromised patterns for demanding "her" share, even when it was not appropriate. The siblings succeeded to resolve the conflict and restored their relationship.

Manipulative psychological tricks of a charismatic mediator helped the siblings to resolve their conflict and reestablish their relationship. However, there are different ways to analyze the negotiating problem and approach the conflict. Different mediators will probably use different methods to cope with the dispute. They might have succeeded or failed. Moreover, a charismatic mediator, who so remarkably succeeded to lead Solution-Focused Negotiation in one case, might fail in a different one.

Mediators are human leaders. And human leaders are limited. Moses, the greatest biblical prophet, did not enter the holy land because the Israelites needed a different kind of leader (Joshua). After the Second World War, Churchill—who played a critical role in saving the world during the war—was replaced. Great Britain probably needed a different kind of leadership. In our context, the questions are: Who is the ideal visionary mediator? How can we find him or her? How can we invite a super mediator to resolve different kinds of conflicts involving different types of people?

Since we do not have good answers to these questions, we need to approach the problem from a different angle of vision. The more practical question is: How can we construct the social conditions that enable ordinary mediators to become visionary ones?

The goal of this book is to pave the way for building an effective and constructive Solution-Focused Negotiation that is not entirely dependent on the skills of human mediators. The framework of the interaction, the rules of the negotiating game and computer technology (support system) can help human mediators substantially improve their performance. The main purpose is to build the conditions that help ordinary intermediaries become visionary mediators.

Concluding Remarks

Solution-Focused Negotiation rests on three pillars: *Transformation, Practicality and Discovery*. This chapter focused on the first pillar—Transformation. The following chapters introduce the other two pillars.

We saw that four elements are necessary to transform conflicting parties into a negotiating cooperative:

Motivation to solve the conflict by peaceful means.
Rules for constructive talks.
A **Platform** for operating the cooperative.
Visionary mediators to lead the negotiation.

The Transformation pillar—turning the opposing parties into a negotiation cooperative—provides the framework and structure for the negotiation. The purpose is to commit the parties to negotiate their differences in good faith. However, commitment of the parties to the process—as important as is—is not enough to guarantee a successful interaction. Building a negotiation cooperative does not ensure constructive, pragmatic and useful talks.

The first pillar—Transformation—describes the building blocks of a negotiation cooperative. The two other pillars—Practicality and Discovery—focus on the content of the negotiation process. The three pillars are complementary. They are designed to build a productive negotiation cooperative that has a life of its own.

An ideal negotiation cooperative is not dependent on the good will and talent of negotiators and mediators. For example, a "visionary mediator" is a concept and not a specific human being. The challenge is to turn an 'ordinary person' into a 'super mediator'.

Our project is to examine the theoretical performance of an 'ideal negotiation cooperative' and build a 'real-life negotiation cooperative' that functions and operates to reach negotiated agreements that benefit the parties.

Notes

1. See Kant (1983).
2. Huntington (2006, 9–10).
3. Mitchell (1999, 20).
4. Zartman (2000) and Pruitt (2007).
5. Compare to Buchanan (2001), Hayek (1967) and Vanberg (2005).
6. See Kahneman (2013).
7. https://geneva-accord.org/.
8. http://mindsofpeace.org/.
9. Kelman (1996).

References

Buchanan, James M. 2001. *Moral Science and Moral Order*, Vol. 17 of *The Collected Works of James M. Buchanan.* Indianapolis: Liberty Fund.
Hayek, Friedrich August. 1967. *Studies in Philosophy, Politics and Economics.* Chicago: University of Chicago Press.
Huntington, Samuel P. 2006. *Political Order in Changing Societies.* New Haven: Yale University Press.
Kahneman, Daniel. 2013. *Thinking, fast and slow.* New York: Farrar, Straus and Giroux.
Kant, Immanuel. 1983. *Perpetual peace and other essays on politics, history, and morals.* Translated, with intro by Ted Humphrey, Indianapolis: Hackett Publishing Company.
Kelman, Herbert C. 1996. Negotiation as interactive problem solving. *International Negotiation: A Journal of Theory and Practice*, 1 (1): 99-123.
Mitchell, George John.1999. *Making Peace.* New York, NY: Alfred A. Knopf.
Pruitt, Dean. 2007. Readiness theory and the Northern Ireland conflict. *American Behavioral Scientist*, 50 (11): 1520-1541.
Vanberg, Viktor J. 2005. Market and State: The Perspective of Constitutional Political Economy. *Journal of Institutional Economics*, 1 (1): 23-49.
Zartman, I. William. 2000. Ripeness: The Hurting Stalemate and Beyond, in Paul C. Stern & Daniel Druckman (Eds.), *International Conflict Resolution after the Cold War.* Washington: National Academy Press: 225-250.

6

Practicality

Focusing on Practical Solutions to a Negotiable Problem

Binary Trap

Negotiation often starts with clashes between different demands. The opposing sides only see a binary problem. A binary problem permits only two options—right or wrong, yes or no, fair or unfair, black or white. Many conflicts start with binary problems. Each party sees only two possible options—my position or yours.

Binary problems are not negotiable. They leave no room for discussing a wide range of possibilities and negotiating 'objective' criteria to evaluate each of them: Should we get divorce? Do we have a good business plan? Is Benjamin Netanyahu a good Prime Minister for Israel?

Binary problems tend to lead to clashes between viewpoints, positions and demands. Their structure initiates, fuels and inflames conflicts. Binary problems often lead to frustrated debates and block possibilities for constructive negotiation.

However, as strange as it seems, we can look at binary problems as an opportunity to involve conflicting parties in Solution-Focused Negotiation. The sharp contrast between the two opposing options (for example, black or white) enables the sophisticated mediator to better understand the challenge of conflict resolution in the case at stake. Binary problems can be the end of direct clashes and the beginning of constructive negotiation.

One of the main methods of conflict resolution is to modify the problem that inflames the conflict. The art of mediation is the ability to turn binary problems into non-binary problems. A non-binary problem enables the parties to examine different alternative solutions to a challenging situation.

© The Author(s), under exclusive license to Springer Nature Switzerland AG 2024
S. Handelman, *Solution-Focused Negotiation*, Professional Practice in Governance and Public Organizations, https://doi.org/10.1007/978-3-031-52876-7_6

The opposing solutions to a binary problem—such as, "Should we paint the kitchen's walls black or white?"—can be the beginning of the negotiating game. The opposing solutions to a binary problem (black or white) could be the opening positions in negotiating a non-binary problem—"What is the most suitable color for the kitchen's walls?". My request for black and my wife's demand for white can be the starting point in negotiating the shades of gray.

The contrasting options in a binary problem—black or white—could be the extreme positions in a wide range of possible options—the gray area—in a non-binary problem. Since most of us tend to live in the gray area (between the extremes), the change from a binary problem to a non-binary one enables practical talks. It can help turning a frustrated debate into a constructive problem-solving interaction. Let me demonstrate.

A married couple faces a major crisis in their family life. They consider getting a divorce or containing the crisis and continue their marriage. They see a binary problem in front of them—marriage or divorce. If each one of them advocates a different option, they can find themselves locked in a hopeless frustrating debate. In certain countries, this clash is a proven recipe to a bitter conflict that can have negative consequences on their quality of life.

True, it takes two to make peace and it takes only one to ruin a relationship. In theory, if one of the parties wishes to get a divorce, then separation seems to be inevitable. However, the reality is not so simple. There are countries, like Israel, where there is no clear separation between church (synagogue) and state. In these countries, getting a divorce can be extremely difficult if one of the parties insists on continuing the marriage.

Marriage or divorce is a serious decision. It has an impact on the quality of life of other people beyond the couple. For example, it has a major impact on the lives of the couple's children. The children factor can influence the decision of each one of the parties. In order to reach a better decision, it is recommended to the couple to consider the following question: Are marriage and divorce the only viable options?

Changing the binary problem (marriage or divorce) to a non-binary problem can help the parties cope with the situation. A sophisticated mediator can help the parties replace the binary problem—"Should we remain married or get a divorce?"—with a non-binary question—"What are we going to do with our marriage?".

The non-binary question opens a wide range of possibilities. The two options of the binary question (marriage or divorce) become the extremes of a wide range of options in the non-binary question. They can be the starting point for discussing the middle way (the gray area).

The middle way includes imagined and unimagined possibilities, such as: open marriage, shared-home/separate-life, or separate-homes/shared-life. Discussing the different options enabled the couple to better understand the challenge that they are facing. They can reach a wiser decision and get ready for a major change in their life. The same mechanism can be applied in political conflicts.

Israelis and Palestinians, often enough, tend to be caught in a binary problem. They see only two possibilities to settle the conflict. Most of them seem to believe that the main question is—Which is the optimal solution to the conflict "One-State Solution" or "Two-State Solution"? The "One-State Solution" means socio-political marriage between Israelis and Palestinians. The "Two-State Solution" means socio-political divorce between the two identity groups.

Israeli and Palestinian political elites have been engaged in endless binary discussions that compare the advantages and disadvantages of these two options. However, changing the binary problem to a non-binary one reveals different possibilities that most of them have not been seriously explored. Non-binary questions could be: What is the optimal solution to the Israeli-Palestinian conflict? How to build the foundations for a long-lasting and stable peace? What can we learn from other cases of intractable conflict that have been transformed or resolved?

Changing a binary problem to a non-binary one opens new possibilities for discussion. It enables the parties to examine the problem of peace and conflict from a fresh perspective. The two possible options in the binary question—"One-State Solution" and "Two-State Solution"—become the extreme possibilities in a wide range of options (the gray area between the extremes), such as different combinations of unification and separation. For example, Confederation (two cooperative states) and Federation (one state that contains different autonomic units). Moreover, a serious discussion of different possibilities raises doubts if the extremes—"One-State Solution" and "Two-State Solution"—are viable options.

A strict "One-State Solution" means socio-political marriage between the two peoples (Israelis and Palestinians). And if the Israelis do not wish to marry Palestinians—they are afraid to lose the only Jewish state in the world—than marriage is not a viable option. A strict "Two-State Solution" means divorce—a complete separation. However, hermetic separation between Israelis and Palestinians is also not a viable option in this situation. Contact between Israelis and Palestinians is unavoidable in almost all dimensions of social life. The fate of the two communities—whether they like it or not—is intertwined in almost every dimension—geographically, economically, emotionally, etc.

The non-binary problem gives the parties a sense of proportion. It enables them to better understand the complex challenge of conflict resolution. In the Israeli-Palestinian case, it could lead negotiators to the inevitable conclusion—peace has to be made, built and kept (peacemaking, peacebuilding and peacekeeping). They will have to take these three elements of peace into their calculations.[1]

Distinguishing binary and non-binary problems is a main challenge in conflict resolution—"the Negotiating Problem". Let me approach this topic from a different perspective.

Resolvable and Irresolvable Conflicts

Conflict, according to this book, is a problem with various demands for its resolution. Solution-Focused Negotiation is an intensive attempt to reach a practical and enforceable solution to the conflict. Conflicts that belong to the mental sphere—such as viewpoints, beliefs and feelings—are non-negotiable. It is impossible to find an objective criterion to measure our thoughts, beliefs and feelings.

It is impossible to measure how much you "really" care for me, the extent of your belief in God and the level of your impression from a work of art. Conflicts that belong to the mental sphere are binary problems—love versus hate, belief versus non-belief, impressed or not impressed—and binary problems are not negotiable.

The art of conflict resolution is to transform non-negotiable problems into negotiable ones. Fisher and Ury, in their bestseller book *Getting to Yes*, pointed out that the crux of the matter is to change the 'negotiating problem'. They suggested that the negotiating problem be presented in terms of interests instead of positions. This transformation, according to their perception, opens a wide range of possible solutions.

Conflicting parties, like almost all human beings, have different kinds of interests. For example, spouses wish to remain married and still have the maximum degree of freedom; business people aspire to maximize their profits and, at the same time, maintain good and cooperative relationships with their competitors; leaders wish to have unlimited political power and yet lead a democratic country.

According to Fisher and Ury, there are various ways to satisfy different interests. Presenting a conflict in terms of interests enables one to bypass the binary problem. It opens a wide range of possibilities for discussing problems and reaching agreements of mutual benefit.

It is impossible to negotiate religious beliefs. People cannot negotiate the question: "How much belief in God is required for building and maintaining a decent society?" Non-negotiable questions lead to the Binary Trap—Belief in the providence of God or Not. However, human beings can negotiate their interests and needs: "How to build a decent social order (rules and institutions) that enables religious and secular people to live in peace and harmony?".

Interests are motivating vehicles for actions. In principle, according to Fisher and Ury, it is possible to find a variety of practical options to satisfy interests or, at least, part of them. As the next example demonstrates, resolving disputes by negotiating interests can be a multidimensional puzzle.

The fiancée of a student of mine became a religious Jew. He started demanding that his future wife (my student) believe in God and begin living an Orthodox life. My student refused. The couple were caught in a binary game that made their life miserable. When he became persistent and insisted that she change her way of life—dressing, habits and behavior—she became more reluctant to the idea. Any attempt to discuss the topic led to anger, confrontations, fights and frustration.

My student and her fiancée's mother motivated the future groom to participate in Online Solution-Focused Negotiation. A good friend of my student led the negotiation (the acting mediator) and I served as a secret advisor (Back-door mediation).

The acting mediator emphasized that both parties wish to continue the relationship and get married (a shared interest). Moreover, it turned out that the lady (the future bride) is willing to consider the idea of living religious life. She wishes to do it at her own tempo and without any pressure and coercion.

The future groom understood that he operates against his own best interest. The more he pushes his girlfriend to observe the Jewish commandments, the more she becomes defensive and advocates a secular position. His insistence creates the opposite of his desired result.

The mediator asked the couple to choose one important topic for the negotiation. She recommended to choose an issue that leads to constant confrontations in their daily life. They chose to discuss and negotiate the lady's clothing.

The boyfriend demanded that his girlfriend dress as a strict orthodox Jew (for example, conservative skirts and shirts with long sleeves). She refused. She even rejected his "practical" and "generous" offer to go shopping for clothes together. She wanted to prevent fights in the clothing shops. Unfortunately, they were caught in the binary trap—Jewish orthodox clothes or (by orthodox standards) immodest clothes.

It is quite clear that between the extremes—Jewish orthodox and immodest clothes—there is a wide range of options. The binary game, conflict between viewpoints and positions, made the parties blind to other decent options. In contrast, focusing on interests and needs could lead the parties to consider different possible options that were blocked in the usual furious binary discussion.

The mediator reminded the couple that they respect one another and they wish to get married. They have a shared interest to live a relaxed, enjoyable and satisfactory life together. Each of them has an interest to make the other happy.

The mediator maneuvered the parties to search for practical solutions that address their interests and needs on a basis of reciprocity. This method enabled them to overcome the binary trap. The discussion focused upon a pragmatic non-binary problem—What kinds of clothes could be comfortable for the lady without offending the religious feelings of her boyfriend?

They reached an agreement. They agreed that she will not wear tight pants and she will buy shirts with long sleeves. They were quite satisfied with the result.

Solution-Focused Negotiation is neither a courtroom nor a psychological treatment. It is a deal-making instrument and relationship-building device. A successful interaction—that addresses the interests, needs and fears of the parties—can set up the conditions for constructive relationships in various areas.

Research shows that adopting a keystone habit—such as quitting smoking, eating healthy food and showing respect to your spouse—can have a major impact on behaviors, attitudes and relationships in many dimensions.[2] In our case, the focus on the interests and needs of the couple enabled them to cope with a problem that created ongoing tensions in their relationship. They reached a negotiated agreement of mutual advantage. However, we should be very careful not to exaggerate and overestimate the power of Solution-Focused Negotiation.

Perhaps, the interaction helped the couple learn how to overcome difficult moments in their relationship. They learned to cope with disputes and ask for help in difficult and stressful situations. But there is also the possibility that the differences between their views, aspirations and lifestyles are irreconcilable. In this case, separation will probably be inevitable. And a peaceful separation could also be a desirable outcome.

Conflicts of Interests

Conflict is a problem with different demands for its resolution. The parties are locked in a binary discussion. Solution-Focused Negotiation is an intensive attempt of the opposing parties to reach practical and enforceable agreements that settle the conflict by peaceful means.

Conflicts that belong to the mental sphere—such as, viewpoints, beliefs and feelings—are non-negotiable. It is impossible to measure viewpoints, exchange beliefs and enforce emotions. Often enough, these conflicts lead to the Binary Trap—my position versus yours. The inevitable result is a dealbreaker.

Fisher and Ury, in their classic book *Getting to Yes*, introduced an attractive method to overcome such complications. They suggested transforming 'positional bargaining' into 'interests-based negotiation'. Each party has interests that can be satisfied in various ways. The focus on interests can convert a non-negotiable problem (a binary problem) into a negotiable problem (a non-binary problem). Is this the ultimate method for salvation?

The authors of *Getting to Yes* introduced an innovative idea. It worked in many cases that were considered to be desperate. However, there are conflicting situations where one of the main problems is the interests of at least one of the major players in the confrontation. His or her interest in sabotaging any possibility to reach a negotiated agreement of mutual benefit becomes a strategic barrier for conflict resolution.

Following the 2022 Israeli legislative election, the new minister of justice, Yariv Levin, introduced a series of major changes to the judicial system and the balance of powers between the three authorities—the executive (government), legislative (parliament) and judicial. The Israeli public was divided between supporters and opponents of the plan. The supports claimed that the proposed change is a necessary judicial reform. The opponents argued that it is a revolution for dictatorship. They were caught in a binary zero-sum game.

Mass public protests led to a pause in the change process. Representatives of the coalition and the opposition parties in the Israeli parliament started to negotiate solutions to the dispute under the auspice of the Israeli President's office. They searched for a compromise regarding the government's plan to initiate substantial changes in the operation of the judicial system. The negotiation collapsed. It was clear to major figures in the opposition camp that the Israeli Prime Minister, Benjamin Netanyahu, was responsible for the failure. He had a clear interest to block any attempt to reach a negotiated solution.

This sad episode—that has torn Israeli society apart—has happened during the corruption trail of the Israeli Prime Minister, Benjamin Netanyahu.

Netanyahu was charged with breach of trust and accepting bribes. The opponents of the government's efforts to overhaul the judicial system claimed that Mr. Netanyahu had a clear interest to sabotage the negotiation. Controlling the judicial system—which could be a direct result of the proposed changes—was the only way for him to escape conviction. According to this view, the interest of Mr. Netanyahu was a strategic barrier to negotiation and conflict resolution. His interest is non-negotiable and cannot help the parties overcome the Binary Trap.

I do not know if this analysis is true, partially true or completely false. I do know that conflicts of interests in politics can lead to disaster.

Leaders Who Did Not Know How to Negotiate

In 1947, the Bengal area was divided into two zones—part went to India and part went to Pakistan. The intention was to resolve tensions between Muslims and Hindus. However, the people in East and West Pakistan, who basically share the same religion, were separated economically, culturally, and by 1,000 miles of Indian territory.

The new united Pakistan came into being as a parliamentary democracy. However, it suffered from the classic symptoms of a weak state: blatant corruption, institutional dysfunction and insufficient dispute resolution mechanisms. As a result, the army came to play a dominant role in the political order of the new state. By 1958, when the country was in a state of chaos, the army took control and Pakistan became a military dictatorship.

The dominant economy was in East Pakistan and 55% of the population lived there. However, the army centralized its power in West Pakistan and the country was dominated by West Pakistani people. The East Pakistan inhabitants believed they experienced political and economic exploitation and discrimination. They constantly demanded establishment of power sharing mechanisms.

The tension between the two wings of Pakistan grew to a real danger of civil strife. To cope with the problem, the dictator promised to return the country to civilian rule. In 1970, he set up a general election for a constituent assembly. The elections were based on the principle of 'one-person, one-vote'.

Surprisingly, the Awami League (AL)—the dominant party in East Pakistan—won the election and gained an absolute majority in the constituent assembly. Their first reaction was a firm demand to respect and implement the results of the election. They asked to form a constitution and establish a central government. The leadership of the Pakistan People's Party (PPP)—which was the dominant party of West Pakistan—and the military elites refused. They did not want to cede power to the Awami League.

The two sides were caught in a binary game—the Eastern versus the Western positions. Analyzing the conflict in terms of interests was no help. The difference between the interests, needs and aspirations of the two sides played a major role in inflaming the conflict.

The conflict between East and West Pakistan seems to grow out of contrasting interests and needs. The East Pakistani side aspired to have a province with "maximum autonomy, that is to say, maximum legislative, administrative and financial power".[3] The West Pakistani side and the military leaders wanted to preserve their dominance and remain in control of the country. They wished to have a strong unitary state—with one governmental system and one economy—that could maintain a tough policy against India.

The two sides would have agreed to form a Federation, which includes a central government and two regional provinces. The conflict centered around the type of federation. The East side wanted the regional provinces to have maximum autonomy. The West side wanted the regional provinces to have minimum autonomy.

Yahya Khan, the military dictator, Sheikh Mujibur Rahman, the leader of the Awami League (East Pakistan), and Zulfikar Ali Bhutto, the leader of PPP (West Pakistan) met to negotiate the constitution of Pakistan. Each side prepared a default option in case of a dealbreaker. In the language of negotiation scholars, each side prepared its own BATNA (Best Alternative to a Negotiated Agreement).

Mujib's default option was secession and turn East Pakistan into an independent country. Bhutto's default option was maintaining the status quo—the domination of the West in a unitary state. The lack of trust led to a zero-sum game. Each proposal of one side was perceived by the other as a step toward implementing its worst nightmare.

Bhutto saw Mujib's proposals as a move toward the division of Pakistan. Mujib saw Bhutto's proposals as an attempt to maintain the status quo (domination by the West) under a different disguise. They were engaged in a conversation of the deaf.

Both Bhutto and Mujib overestimated their leverage and disregarded the power and determination of the other. This is a well-known cognitive bias. It is a proven recipe for disaster.

Bhutto was supported by the military elite. Mujib was supported by the East Pakistani people. Bhutto knew that the army is ready to use military force to prevent any attempt to divide Pakistan. Mujib knew the determination of the East Pakistani people for autonomy and their ability to resist any attempt to maintain the status quo by force. Neither Mujib nor Bhutto fully grasped the potential for upheaval, disturbance and chaos that waited for them if they fail to reach an acceptable negotiated agreement.

The negotiation stalled and the East Pakistani public discontent reached a fever pitch. East Pakistani elites seemed to have no other choice but to demand outright autonomy and eventual secession. This was the trigger that led the army to abandon negotiation and instigate a crackdown.

The year of 1971, which started with the hope of democracy in Pakistan, ended with one of the bloodiest conflicts in the Cold War era. Following the collapse of the negotiation, the army launched Operation Searchlight—a military attack on the East Pakistani national movement. The intention was to stop any effort to divide Pakistan. The operation, unintendedly, developed into a full-scale bloody civil war with enormous casualties. One of the main results of the tragic violent confrontation was the creation of an independent East Pakistan, known as Bangladesh.

Bhutto and Mujib were locked in a binary game. Each one believed that he had power, leverage and momentum. This tragic mistake led to a disaster. What could have been done differently? How could the civil war have been avoided? What were the possibilities to break the negotiation deadlock?

It is difficult to know. We can assume that the fatal mistake was to leave the negotiation in the hands of irresponsible politicians. The involvement of different elements of the opposing societies—such as the public and a wide range of political elites—in the efforts to resolve the conflict might have led to different results.

In contrast to the Pakistani leadership, the leaders of South Africa and Northern Ireland understood their limitations during their revolutionary peacemaking processes in the 1990s. In both cases, visionary leaders—such as Nelson Mandela and Willem de Klerk in South Africa—understood the importance of public involvement and support in the struggle for change. They established multiparty congresses that invited a wide range of political representatives to discuss, debate and negotiate solutions to their conflict. These congresses teetered from one crisis to another and did not show any signs of progress for quite a long time. However, they eventually gave the peace process a life of its own and prepared the ground for engaging the leaderships in effective Solution-Focused Negotiation. The results were agreements that gained public support.[4]

In deep-rooted political conflicts, Solution-Focused Negotiation often cannot bring peace and stability by itself. There is a need for supportive mechanisms that can push the peace process forward. It is necessary to prepare the ground for using the intensive conflict resolution mechanisms of Solution-Focused Negotiation.

Political leaders are human beings. As Tversky and Kahneman demonstrated, again and again, human judgment and decision-making are subject to cognitive biases, such as overconfidence. Cognitive biases can lead to a Binary Trap in almost all types of conflict, from family disputes to politics.

Cognitive Biases and the Binary Trap

Conflicts often start with genuine substantial problems. For example: What is the most desirable environment for raising our children? How should we allocate state resources for the benefit of the citizens? What is the most effective strategy for our company in a competitive market?

We can assume that rational human beings—if they have complete information—could solve most of their conflicts by peaceful means. However, we are not living in an ideal world. In our imperfect world, psychology complicates situations of conflict beyond imagination. Disputing parties can be involved in entrenched conflicts for quite a long time. The continuation of the conflict can have a negative effect on the interests of the parties and may cause them a great deal of suffering and misery.

Psychologists, like Freud, demonstrated that people often operate against their own best interests. They do it in a systematic way, even when it seriously damages their quality of life and well-being. The question is: Why?

Scholars came to a conclusion that we have, at least, two systems of thinking. They presented different theories and named the two systems differently—conscious and unconscious, rational and irrational, intellectual and emotional. Tversky and Kahneman focused on cognitive biases to demonstrate the impact of the emotional system on our irrational patterns of behavior or, to be more precise, on patterns that seem to be irrational.

Cognitive biases are automatic patterns of brain processes that create distortion in our situational perspective, analysis and judgment. In Daniel Kahneman's terminology, a trigger stimulates an instinctive reaction of the irrational mind (system 1), which leads to a systematic error in thinking and judgment of the systematic mind (system 2). A well-known example is the sunk-cost fallacy.

The sunk-cost fallacy enhances the likelihood of making an unreasonable decision to continue investing resources in a losing account. People are inclined to continue investing time, effort and financial resources in projects with bad returns, even when better options are available. This irrational tendency affects the decision-making, judgment and behavior of human beings from all walks of life.

Research shows that ordinary people, experienced businessmen and professional politicians make decisions that involve the sunk-cost fallacy. For example, I repeatedly took my car to the same repair shop with the same problem that they do not know how to fix even though they kept charging me money for their useless trial-and-error efforts; Business people continue investing money in a bad project, even when the market offers better opportunities; Politicians continue to push a political program—which they had planned for many years—even when it becomes clear that implementing the program causes more harm than benefit to society.

Following Daniel Kahneman's analysis, in all of these cases our mental account (system 1) is deficient. The bad investment leads us to feel disappointed, frustrated and defeated. Our prestige is damaged. We are inclined to do more of the same—continue to invest in a bad project—in order to recoup our loss. Unfortunately, we usually achieve the opposite result.[5]

It is difficult to leave a negative balance in our mental account and move on. It is difficult to admit that we made a bad investment and further expenditure in the same direction might worsen the situation. In other words, the rational thinking (system 2) finds it difficult to take control and restrain the irrational thinking (system 1). As the next example demonstrates, cognitive biases—such as the sunk-cost fallacy—can inflame conflicts. They can lead the parties straight to the Binary Trap. However, a proper setting of Solution-Focused Negotiation can lead the parties to help each other overcome this trap.

Tension in a family relationship is a quite common phenomenon. A married couple can find themselves involved in a bitter conflict, even when they care for each other deep in their heart. They do not see separation as a viable option but they find it difficult to contain the conflict. Ongoing confrontations over the same issue create an unpleasant atmosphere at home. This happened to one of my former students.

The dispute centered around their family house. The wife wanted to continue living in their home. The husband insisted on moving to a different house in a different location. They were caught in a binary dispute: "Should we stay in our house or should we leave?".

The wife emphasized the financial resources and the mental and physical effort they invested in renovating their home. For her, changing their place of living—after such a huge investment—was not an option. Her husband claimed that the maintenance of the house is too expensive (financially), too difficult (physically) and too exhausting (mentality). He insisted they could find a decent, affordable and convenient house in a different location and improve their quality of life.

Their emotional mind (system 1) played a major role in their attempt to discuss this topic. They did not really listen to one another. They were caught in a frustrated binary "debate"—to sell or not to sell—with no light at the end of this dark tunnel.

In the framework of Tversky and Kahneman, her arguments indicate she got trapped in the sunk-cost fallacy. The deficit in her emotional balance (system 1)—she kept emphasizing their huge investment in renovating the house—distorted her rational thinking (system 2). She was not ready and willing to critically examine her position and explore other options. Her husband was dragged into a frustrated binary debate.

Often, a party that advocates an extreme position in an argument instinctively leads the other party to adopt the other extreme. Her extreme and uncompromising demand to stay in their house led him to take the other extreme—changing their residence is necessary for a happy life. He presented the house as a bottomless investment. He preferred to risk moving to another house than to continue living in an unaffordable house whose maintenance constantly damaged their well-being.

Moving to another house has a different meaning to each of them. The wife emphasized the loss of investment, while her husband emphasized the opportunity to get rid of a bad investment and improve their quality of life. Both of them care for the well-being of the family and wanted to solve the dispute. They agreed to participate in Online Solution-Focused Negotiation.

During the negotiation, one of the husband's first moves was to declare that he respects his wife and appreciates her point of view. Accordingly, he is willing to freeze the idea of selling the house for three months. In the interim period, they will examine, explore and calculate their options together.

After the negotiation ended, the wife (my student) asked to meet with me. She told me that the turning point in the negotiation was her husband's declaration and gesture. His willingness to freeze any discussion on selling the house for three months showed her that he really cares for her. This kind of respect and empathy motivated her to critically examine her initial position and explore different possibilities and options.

As a response to the husband's first move, the wife suggested that during the interim period (three months):

1. She will arrange the house differently to make it more comfortable to her husband;
2. Together with her husband, they will examine 5 alternative houses in a different location.

Her proposal was the outline of their negotiated agreement.

In conclusion, the husband's empathic move seems to balance the deficit in the mental account of his wife, caused by the sunk cost. Together, they succeeded in overcoming the Binary Trap. They replaced the binary question—"Should we change our home?"—with a non-binary question—"What is the best way to reach a wise decision about our place of living?".

They reached an interim negotiated agreement. They agreed on practical actions that would help them reach a joint decision about their place of living during the next three months. After the interim period (three months), they needed to reach a final binary decision—to stay or leave. I was curious to know what they did do with their house.

A few months later, the wife (my student) sent me a massage. She wrote that their younger son is manipulating them (crying, insisting and demanding) to move to a house near his school. She believed that they do not have much choice but to sell the house and buy another one near the school.

As an old Jewish saying goes: "the work of the righteous is done by others".

Concluding Remarks

Our social life invites challenging situations. Conflicts tend to emerge when parties look at the challenge in a binary form—black or white, good or bad, yes or no. The parties see only two options to cope with the challenge that has an impact on their relationship—"my position or yours". They often do not identify a negotiable difference.

In contrast, there is another way to cope with a challenging situation. The challenge can be introduced in a non-binary way. A non-binary form offers a wide range of options to cope with the problem. It opens the possibility to negotiate different solutions. A critical element in the art of conflict resolution is the ability to transform the binary presentation of a conflicting problem into a non-binary one.

We discussed three methods to transform a binary problem into a non-binary one. Each one of them has advantages and disadvantages:

1. Replacing binary questions with non-binary ones

Conflicts center around the binary presentation of a challenging problem. Binary problems can be introduced by binary questions. Binary questions, often enough, start with "is", "are", "should" or "do". They enable two possible answers. For example:

- Should we get a divorce?
- Is it necessary to provide a financial bonus to employees with innovative ideas?
- Do we have a moral obligation to spread democratic values by aggressive means?

Changing a binary question to a non-binary one enables the parties to discuss a variety of options. It has the potential to transform a binary problem into a non-binary one. Non-binary questions, often enough, start with words like "what" and "how". For example:

- What is the best way to cope with the problems in our marriage?
- How can we motivate our employees to improve their performance?
- How should we spread democratic values in a non-democratic world?

Non-binary questions sketch a multidimensional picture of the conflict and its implications. They help the parties understand the challenges they are facing and enable them to explore possibilities that were blocked in the binary stage. However, it is not always easy to use non-binary questions as an effective conflict resolution tool.

One of the most complicated challenges in Solution-Focused Negotiation is to identify, formulate and present the appropriate non-binary questions.

2. Focus on Interests, Needs and Fears, not Positions

Fisher and Ury pointed out that positional bargaining leads to the Binary Trap. The opposing parties become entrenched in their positions. Each party is not ready, willing or able to listen to the other side and critically examine his or her position. To cope with the problem, Fisher and Ury suggested focusing on the interests of the parties and not on their positions.

People have various interests in various dimensions. They have conflicting, complementary and other kinds of interests. In addition, there are various ways to satisfy interests. Therefore, the focus on interests can open different possibilities for negotiation and help the parties avoid the Binary Trap.

Fisher and Ury describe a classic example in the history of negotiation. They focus on a central issue in the 1978 Camp David Summit that led to a peace treaty between Egypt and Israel. I described and analyzed the summit in Chap. 3.

One of the most difficult issues was the Sinai Peninsula. Each side claimed the area for itself. They were caught in the Binary Trap.

A careful analysis of their interests enabled this complication to be overcome. The Egyptians were motivated by identity considerations. The Israelis were motivated by security concerns. The shift from positions to interests avoided the Binary Trap. It enabled the parties to shift a binary problem—"Who should control the area?" to a non-binary one—"How to address the interests, fears and needs of each side on a basis of reciprocity?".

Fisher and Ury presented an innovative idea to cope with different types of conflicts—from family disputes to politics. However, they did not provide a satisfactory method to cope with situations where the interest of, at least, one of the parties becomes a problem. There are conflicting situations when a central player in the confrontation has a clear interest to block any possibility to reach a negotiated agreement of mutual benefit. In these situations, the interest of the spoiler becomes a strategic barrier to negotiation, peacemaking and conflict resolution.

3. Suggesting practical solutions

Scholars of Brief Solution-Focused Therapy claimed that therapeutic sessions should focus on solutions and not on the problem. We can use the same useful insight in Solution-Focused Negotiation. Suggesting practical solutions to cope with a distressful situation that triggers conflict can create a change.

The focus on practical solutions to a challenging situation can shift attention from the Binary Trap. This change can happen unexpectedly and without the attention of the parties. There is no need to formulate a non-binary question (method 1), and it is not necessary to analyze the interests, needs and fears of the parties (method 2) to reach such an effect. The potential of such a strategic move to create a change was demonstrated in the description of the family dispute over their place of living.

The wife and her husband were caught in a Binary Trap (to sell or not sell the house). Suddenly, out of nowhere, the husband suggested a practical plan to reach a wise decision. His unexpected move enabled the parties to escape the Binary Trap. They started operating as a team that struggles to solve a joint problem—"What is the most effective way to reach an optimal decision and maintain a good atmosphere at home?" This was an unexpected change in their perspective of the conflict. How did such an astonishing shift happen?

In conflicting situations, the parties are often entrenched in their positions. They are not ready, willing or able to listen, think and explore new ideas. The husband, in our case, used empathy to bring his wife to consider his idea. This move shifted the discussion to a problem that could be solved.

In general, the tactic used to introduce an innovative idea is no less important than the idea itself. It seems that using manipulative elements—such as tactical empathy—is necessary to make an impact in situations of conflict. However, the use of manipulative elements for a "good" cause can have social costs. It might have a negative impact on the relationship in the long run. Unfortunately, there are no free lunches.

The shift from a binary problem to a non-binary one is an important element on the road to successfully conclude Solution-Focused Negotiation. However, it does not guarantee success. Unfortunately, the negotiation can deteriorate again into an endless binary debate or, in the terminology of Fisher and Ury, (frustrated) positional bargaining.

Interesting and important questions are: Why can a negotiable conflict turn into a non-negotiable conflict during a Solution-Focused Negotiation? Why can constructive negotiation—a joint search for alternative options to satisfy interests and needs—turn into a frustrating debate (a clash between viewpoints)? Why can a Solution-Focused Negotiation that seems to be on the right track suddenly, without any notice, reach a deadlock?

A major reason for such a disruption is lack of knowledge. The negotiation reaches a turning point, a point where the parties need to progress. But they do not know how to take the negotiation to the next level.

The parties are committed to the negotiating process (transformation). They try to focus on practical solutions to a negotiable problem (practicality). But they do not have the knowledge to overcome substantial obstacles and bring the negotiation to a successful conclusion. They reach a deadlock.

This is a common phenomenon that appears in almost any type of negotiation, from family disputes to politics. A married couple do not know how to divide the household chores for the benefit of the family; business partners do not have any idea how to overcome a financial crisis in the stock market; and rival policymakers do not have any clue how to cope with a major national security problem.

The helplessness—the inability to progress—becomes a dealbreaker. It leads to anger, frustration and despair. The result is deterioration to old familiar destructive habits—blame, accusation and slander. In Daniel Kahneman's terminology, system 1 (the impulsive mind) of the negotiating parties leads them to behave and operate against to their own best interests and needs.

To overcome the obstacle and prevent a crisis, the negotiators need a constructive game changer. A constructive game changer illuminates the interaction in a different light. It enables the parties to examine the situation from a fresh perspective.

To conclude, it is quite common for Solution-Focused Negotiation to reach a turning point. The turning point could be a dealbreaker (a destructive game changer) or a deal-maker (a constructive game changer). The ability to discover or create key constructive game changers can be a masterpiece. This is the topic of the next chapter.

Notes

1. See Handelman (2019) and Handelman (2017).
2. Duhigg (2012).
3. https://www.icj.org/wp-content/uploads/1972/06/Bangladesh-events-East-Pakistan-1971-thematic-report-1972-eng.pdf.
4. See, for example, Handelman (2021).
5. Compare to Kahneman (2013).

References

Duhigg, Charles. 2012. *The power of habit: Why we do what we do in life and business.* New York: Random House.

Handelman, Sapir. 2017. Peacemaking, peacebuilding and peacekeeping: the challenge of change in the Israeli– Palestinian conflict. *Israel Affairs*, 23(3): 453–467.

Handelman, Sapir. 2019. Peace Revolution as a Three-Dimensional Process – The Israeli-Palestinian Case, in Maigul Nugmanova, Heimo Juhani Mikkola, Alexander Rozanov and Valentina Komleva (eds.) *Education, Human Rights and Peace in Sustainable Development*, London: IntechOpen. https://www.intechopen.com/chapters/70302

Handelman, Sapir. 2021. *Elements of Peacemaking Revolutions: Leaders, People and Institutions.* Newcastle upon Tyne: Cambridge Scholars Publishing.

Kahneman, Daniel. 2013. *Thinking, fast and slow.* New York: Farrar, Straus and Giroux.

ns.

7

Discovery
Detecting Key Game Changers

Karl Popper, a great philosopher of science, taught us that "all life is problem solving". Any progress toward a specific goal creates new problems, challenges and complications. Solution-Focused Negotiation constitutes, at least, three stages of a problem-solving process. In the most difficult conflicts, progress from one stage to the next requires key game changers.

Three Types of Game Changers

Solution-Focused Negotiation is usually a three-stage process. Each stage can be challenging. The first challenge is to initiate a negotiating process and turn the opposing parties into a negotiating cooperative. The second challenge is to help the negotiating partners focus on practical solutions to a negotiable problem. The third challenge is to conclude agreements of mutual benefit.

In difficult situations of conflict, advancing from one stage to the next can be a tremendous challenge. Key game changers are often required for progress. The negotiating process—moving from conflict to resolution—becomes a discovery procedure. It becomes the art of discovering, creating or inventing key game changers that enable constructive, efficient and effective progress.

I suggest that we distinguish three types of game changers: **Initiating game changers** enable the initiation of Solution-Focused Negotiation and help create commitment to the process; **Motivating game changers** provide incentives to negotiate in good faith and keep the process alive in difficult moments; and **Resolving game changers** facilitate reaching agreements of mutual benefit and enable successful conclusion of the negotiation.

The dramatic diplomatic offensive of Anwar Sadat—the President of Egypt—on the hardline Israeli government in 1978 is an example of an **initiating game changer** (the first stage). The public announcement of President Sadat that he is willing to come to Jerusalem to speak about peace in the Israeli parliament created the momentum to begin a peace process in a situation that was considered desperate. It was a turning point in the relationship between the two countries that enabled their leaders to engage in Solution-Focused Negotiation.

However, the parties were far from reaching agreements. They faced a strategic barrier. The two leaders held contrasting viewpoints about the desired peace process—a comprehensive Middle East peace (Sadat) versus a separate peace between Egypt and Israel (Begin). These contrasting viewpoints led to frustrating positional bargaining. The summit was in grave danger of collapsing. They needed a **motivating key game changer** to keep the process alive. The turning point was a change in the focus of the negotiation—from positional bargaining to interests-based negotiation.

Both sides had a sincere desire that the summit will succeed. The analysis of their interests, needs and fears created peacemaking opportunities which helped to keep the process alive. For example, one of the most difficult topics was the Sinai Peninsula.

The initial picture was quite gloomy. Each side claimed the area for itself. A careful analysis of the parties' motivations and concerns ("Why do you need the area?") was a game changer. It created problem-solving opportunities. Egyptians viewed the area as an integral part of their identity and history. Israelis saw the area as a security asset. Sinai provided a defensible border for their country. However, the Israeli need for security does not necessarily mean that Israelis must own the Sinai Peninsula. There are other ways to address their security needs and interests.

The solution to the problem of Sinai addressed the interests and needs of both sides, at least to some extent. Egypt gained the area and Israel gained security. Israel gave the area back to Egypt and the two sides agreed to establish security mechanisms to guarantee the safety of Israel. For example, demilitarizing Sinai and establishing an international peacekeeping force.

The focus on the interests, needs and fears of the parties motivated them to continue taking an active part in the summit despite the difficulties. Moreover, it enabled them to resolve one of the most difficult conflicting issues, the Sinai Peninsula. However, it was not enough to successfully conclude the summit. They needed another innovative idea—a **resolving game changer**—to overcome major obstacles to reaching peace agreements.

The idea to conclude two separate agreements was a **resolving game changer**. The two agreements were drafted to address the interests, needs and fears of the opposing parties on a basis of reciprocity. The first agreement—*A Framework for Peace in the Middle East*—addressed the interests of Sadat to lay the foundations for a comprehensive peace in the Middle East. The second agreement—*A Framework for the Conclusion of a Peace Treaty between Egypt and Israel*—addressed the interests of Begin for a separate peace between the two countries. The leaders succeeded in understanding the interests, needs and fears of each other and found a balance between their different motivations.

The main focus of this chapter is the third type of game changer, the **Resolving Game Changer**. The assumption is that disputing parties engaged in a Solution-Focused Negotiation are committed to the process, but they do not know how to proceed and successfully conclude the process. They need a game changer to overcome the deadlock.

Negotiation as a Discovery Procedure

Brief Solution-Focused Therapy is similar to Solution-Focused Negotiation. Both are intensive interactions designed to help human beings cope with problems. Both settings focus on pragmatic solutions to challenges in different areas of our personal and social lives.

Clients come to therapy to find solutions to their problems. They ask for professional help because they cannot cope with their problems by themselves. Nevertheless, one of the basic assumptions in Brief Solution-Focused Therapy is that clients actually do hold the key for resolving their problems. They need help to bypass barriers that prevent their discovery of tools that could lead them to identify and explore practical solutions to their problems.

Key questions in Brief Solution-Focused Therapy are: How did you cope with a similar situation in the past? What did you do to overcome the problem? How could you recreate your actions and adjust them to the new situation?

This basic assumption of Brief Solution-Focused Therapy is valid for certain cases of Solution-Focused Negotiation. In both cases, the clients hold the keys to resolving their problems. Indeed, it seems that Anwar Sadat (the Egyptian President) and Menachem Begin (the Israeli Prime Minister) knew the basic guidelines of a realistic negotiated peace treaty. For example,

Sadat—who emphasized the critical importance of solving the Palestinian problem—did not insist on inviting Palestinian representatives to the negotiating table at the 1978 Camp David Summit. To put it differently, he was ready to conclude a separate peace with Israel.

On the Israeli side, the situation was similar. The Israelis hardly exploited the tourist and financial potential of the Sinai Peninsula. Almost all of the area remained uncultivated during the Israeli regime. In other words, we can assume that Menachem Begin understood that Israel will have to give the area back to Egypt. Nevertheless, the two parties needed a power mediator—a mediator with economic, political and military leverage—to lead the negotiation. And only **resolving game changers** created the difference between success and failure.

A skilled mediator is like an excellent orchestra conductor. A great conductor uses the talents of each musician in the orchestra to create a successful performance. A great mediator motivates negotiators to use their 'practical knowledge' in the deal-making process.

Practical knowledge helps people cope successfully with problems in their daily lives. Practical knowledge is a type of knowledge that is acquired by life experience. Different people have different kinds of practical knowledge.[1]

The practical knowledge of each negotiator enables the conflict to be approached from different directions and dimensions. It is an effective method to discover key game changers. A good mediator can utilize the practical knowledge of each negotiator to produce a joint composition—an agreement that is advantageous to both parties.

In difficult situations of conflict, the ability of the mediator to utilize the practical knowledge of the negotiators can be limited. For example, the parties can be entrenched in their positions, operating against their own best interests, and not using their problem-solving skills. The negotiation reaches a deadlock. Creative and extraordinary thinking is required to save the negotiation. The situation requires insights that are hidden from the parties and the mediator. How can we cope with these difficult situations?

Ideal Mediators and Key Game Changers

Discovering key game changers can be a masterpiece. It requires special talents, such as the ability to listen constructively, broad knowledge, keen perception and creativity. An ideal mediator—like a Machiavellian Prince—is able to provide the right answer at the right time in the right place. How can we help ordinary mediators improve their skills and acquire the abilities of an ideal mediator?

Ideal mediators exist only in fairy tales. Actual mediators are subject to human limitations and have limited information. Chris Voss—a former FBI hostage negotiator—employed a team of assistants to look for and discover key game changers. This enabled him to improve his negotiating skills and abilities. However, most mediators do not have the resources to employ a group of experts to assist them.

It is quite reasonable to assume that each mediator has experience and expertise in certain types of negotiation. The following sections provide insights that could help identify key game changers in different types of negotiations. We intend to show that knowledge of barriers and how to overcome them can improve the performance of mediators.

Three Forms of Negotiation and Key Game Changers

Conflicts are problems with various demands for their resolution. Solution Focused-Negotiation is an intensive attempt to reach practical and enforceable agreements that settle conflicts by peaceful means. However, negotiation is a broad concept. Negotiation means different processes to different people.

Chapter 4 introduces three types of negotiating processes—bargaining, problem-solving and consensus-building. Each of these processes suggests that we approach conflicts from a different perspective. Different key game changers are required to create a turning point in each process and bring the negotiation to a successful conclusion.

To demonstrate the difference between the three types of negotiation, let us take a classic example: two brothers fight over an orange. Each one of them claims the orange for himself and is not willing to compromise. How can we help these brothers solve their problem? Can we help them find a solution of mutual benefit? Is there only one possible negotiated solution that can satisfy both of them?

Bargaining is a competitive form of negotiation. In a bargaining process, the problem of conflict resolution is to transform a destructive competition—tensions, frictions and confrontations—into a constructive contest—negotiating concessions by peaceful means. In the orange example, the bargaining challenge is to transform a clash between maximalist demands (each brother claims the orange for himself) into a peaceful talk about the question—"How can we divide this orange in a manner that will satisfy both sides?".

The simplest intuitive solution is to split the difference. An instinctive compromise is to divide the orange in half. Each brother would get an equal share. How can we make sure that the orange will be divided equally or, at least, to the satisfaction of both sides?

The classic solution is one brother cuts the orange into two pieces, the other brother chooses the piece he wants, and the brother who cuts the orange receives the remaining piece. This formula is designed to prevent any complaints of injustice. Both sides should be satisfied, at least to some extent.[2]

The orange example is a very simple case. In the more difficult cases, one of the main challenges is to identify a negotiable difference. For instance, there are conflicting situations where the object in dispute cannot be divided. Take for example, the famous story from the bible—the Judgment of Solomon.

Two women came to King Solomon. Each of them claimed to be the mother of an infant son. The king gave an order "to split the difference"—to cut the infant into two pieces and give each woman half of the baby. This manipulative trick enabled the king to identify the real mother.

One woman accepted the compromise. The other woman begged the king to not kill the baby even if she did not receive him. King Solomon recognized the woman who wished to keep the baby alive at all costs as the true mother and gave her the child. Negotiation is not court of justice.

Solution-Focused Negotiation is an attempt to reach practical and enforceable agreements that can resolve a conflict to the satisfaction of both sides. In a bargaining process (negotiation as bargaining), the parties need to identify a negotiable difference in order to negotiate a compromise. However, as the biblical Judgment of Solomon story demonstrates, this goal could be a major challenge.

In the most challenging cases of bargaining, identifying a negotiable difference is one of the main difficulties. Key game changers are needed to help the parties overcome the binary debate (my position or yours) and detect a negotiable difference. Is it always necessary?

Negotiation scholars and practitioners have argued that bargaining—a competitive practice of negotiation—is not always the best method to cope with conflicts. And compromise is not necessarily the optimal solution. A problem-solving approach can often bring better results to the conflicting parties.

Problem-solving is a cooperative form of negotiation. The problem-solving approach implies that conflicting parties have a shared problem that they need to solve jointly. The negotiating interaction becomes a problem-solving workshop for Conflict Analysis and Resolution. The analysis focuses upon discovering the interests, needs and fears that cause the parties to engage in unbeneficial conflict. The resolution consists of agreements on mechanisms that satisfy these concerns on a basis of reciprocity.

In the orange example, the key question to ask each party is: "Why do you need the orange?".

In the classic example, it turns out that the parties have different interests and needs. One brother likes oranges and wants to eat the whole orange. The other brother does not like oranges. He wants the orange's peel to use in baking a cake. The discovery of their interests and needs enables the problem to be solved to the satisfaction of both sides. One brother gets the whole orange without the peel. The other brother gets the peel without the orange. Both brothers are happy and satisfied.[3] They should be much more satisfied with this problem-solving solution than with the bargaining process compromise (cut the orange into half). However, social life is not simple. Conflicts can be much more complicated than this classic orange example.

Identifying and addressing the underlying motivations of conflicting parties can often be a momentous task. Key game changers are needed to open possibilities for transforming positional bargaining (at the beginning of the negotiating process) into a problem-solving interaction that addresses the interests, needs and fears of the parties.

Consensus-building focuses on coalition-building. It is the art of building a supportive environment of key players who can have a positive impact on the results of the negotiation. Consensus-building practitioners replace the "How can we resolve this conflict?" question with a "Who should be involved—directly or indirectly—in the negotiating effort?" question.

The orange example reminds me of confrontations between my daughters. There were situations where my older daughter (a teenager) received a present and the younger (five years old) daughter claimed it for herself. They became engaged in a binary conflict ("mine" or "yours").

According to the psychologist Jean Piaget, one reason for the conflict is they have different senses of justice. The older daughter had a teenager's sense of decency, fair-play and sharing. The younger daughter had an infant's sense of justice—"everything belongs to me". Each of them thought with different concepts and perceived the situation differently.

My wife coped with such hopeless situations by making an attractive offer. For example, she offered our younger daughter something she cares about—such as a new Barbie Doll—on condition that she (the younger daughter) stop demanding the gift of the older sister for herself. This tempting offer changed the dynamics of the situation.

Frankly, I cannot evaluate the educational value of my wife's strategy. The example simply demonstrates the potential impact of a key player, who knows the disputing parties very well, on the course of negotiation. In the short run, the conflict was resolved and both daughters were happy.

Disputing parties usually do not live in a vacuum. On the one hand, their conflict can affect the well-being of other people. On the other hand, involving key players—directly or indirectly—in the negotiation can help discover key game changers. The orange example demonstrates both of these results.

On the one hand, there can be a consensus in the family that the orange dispute creates an unpleasant atmosphere at home. On the other hand, involving key players, who know the sensitivities, weaknesses and strengths of the parties, in the effort to resolve the dispute can lead to a turning point. For example, imagine a scenario where the older brother of the disputing parties knows that one of them is a football fan. He can offer to take him to a game on condition that he will let the other brother have the orange.

Negotiations often reach a deadlock. The parties are entrenched in their positions. The mediator does not know how to progress. Involving—directly or indirectly—key players in the negotiation can add fresh perspectives to the interaction. It can lead to a turning point in the process and open possibilities to reach agreements. However, there are two main difficulties in a consensus-building process: (1) Identifying constructive players—Who are the key players that should be involved in the negotiating effort? (2) The method of involvement—How can we involve them in the process?

The consensus-building process is the art of building effective coalitions of pro-negotiating elements that can influence the result of a conflict resolution process. The mediator focuses on the question: "Who should be involved in the negotiation effort and how?".

Bargaining, problem-solving and consensus-building are ideal types of negotiation. In real life, almost any problem-solving interaction involves elements of bargaining and vice versa. In addition, consensus-building processes usually contain elements of bargaining and problem-solving. The schematic distinction between the three types of negotiation enables one to demonstrate the power of key game changers.

Let me demonstrate the interaction between the three forms of negotiation—bargaining, problem-solving and consensus-building—and relevant key game changers.

Positional Bargaining—Islands of Agreement

Bargaining is a competitive form of negotiation. It is a direct clash between opposing demands. We often witness bargaining processes in different areas of our social lives—from family disputes to politics. Neighboring countries have claims for the same territory, siblings compete over the division of their inheritance and each spouse in a divorce process aspires to gain a larger part of their joint property.

The conventional wisdom is that a compromise is needed to resolve the conflict. Splitting the difference can be a good solution to competitive claims. Negotiating a formula to split the difference should be a central motif in a "serious" bargaining process.

In contrast, Chris Voss, a former FBI hostage negotiator, wrote a groundbreaking book with a provocative title: *Never Split the Difference*. Splitting the difference, according to Voss, almost never leads to optimal results. Good negotiators can achieve a much better result than splitting the difference. These results, often enough, can also benefit the opposing parties.[4]

One of the main challenges in bargaining processes is to identify a negotiable difference. Is there any negotiable difference? How do we find it? How can mediators bring parties to identify the negotiable difference and agree on its range? Is there a standard method to construct a negotiable difference? Is it possible to eliminate the difference and how?

Fisher and Ury, in their famous book *Getting to Yes*, taught us that positional bargaining often leads to a dead-end. Each party is entrenched in his or her position. They are not willing, able or ready to seriously and constructively listen to one another and examine different options. The impression is that positional bargaining always leads to irreconcilable differences.

In positional bargaining, the opposing parties are often caught in a binary zero-sum game—my position against yours. This kind of "negotiation" can deteriorate into a debate that ends with slanders, insults and frustration. The parties are not willing, ready or able to identify negotiable differences. Detecting points of agreement within their disagreements—'Islands of Agreement' in the terminology of Gabriella Blum—can be a key game changer. It enables the participants to examine the situation from a fresh perspective and discover negotiable differences. The new discovery modifies the negotiating problem. Let me demonstrate.

We saw in the second chapter that the beginning of the 1978 Camp David Summit did not give much room for optimism. Anwar Sadat—the Egyptian President—and Menachem Begin—the Israeli Prime Minister—held different viewpoints about the desired peace process. Sadat advocated a comprehensive peace in the Middle East. He stated that solving the Palestinian problem is the key to achieve this goal. Begin advocated a separate peace between Egypt and Israel. It seems he believed the Palestinian problem should not be on the negotiation table.

At first sight, the situation looks desperate. The two sides present opposing demands that derive from contradictory viewpoints. They were caught in a binary zero-sum game—comprehensive peace (Sadat) versus separate peace (Begin). Is it possible to find negotiable differences in this situation?

Modifying the picture is necessary to discover negotiable differences. In difficult situations of conflict—where the opposing sides are entrenched in their positions—it is necessary to maneuver the parties to examine the situation from a fresh perspective. A fresh perspective that can open possibilities for negotiation.

One effective method to cope with the binary trap is to search for 'Islands of Agreement'—points of agreement within the disagreements. It can help each party to raise doubts about its position and open new possibilities for negotiation. Can Israel benefit from a comprehensive peace in the Middle East? Can Egypt benefit from a peace treaty with Israel? What are the factors that enable one to examine the possibility that these two positions (comprehensive peace and separate peace) are not necessarily in opposition?

We can assume that, in principle, Begin would agree with Sadat that comprehensive peace in the Middle East is desirable. Sadat would also agree with Begin that a peace treaty between Egypt and Israel is needed. Both of them would agree that solving the Palestinian problem is important and necessary for regional stability.

These 'Islands of Agreement' enabled the leaders to identify negotiable differences. Moreover, it led to an astonishing discovery—the two competitive viewpoints of Sadat and Begin—comprehensive peace *versus* separate peace—can be regarded as complementary—comprehensive peace *and* separate peace. The practical manifestation of this discovery was negotiating two agreements: "Framework for Peace in the Middle East" (Sadat's perspective) and "Framework for the Conclusion of a Peace Treaty between Egypt and Israel" (Begin's perspective).

The idea of negotiating two related agreements was a resolving game changer. It provided new dimensions to the bargaining process, in general, and 'the difference', in particular. The difference in the negotiation of 'comprehensive peace' became dependent on the difference in the talks about the conditions to achieve a 'separate peace'. To put it differently, negotiating two intertwined agreements was based on the principle of reciprocity.

The resolving game changer—two competitive visions that became regarded as complementary—gave the negotiators more flexibility. It enabled them to examine the situation from different perspectives and provided a multidimensional picture of the peacemaking challenge. The new picture illuminated deficiencies in the position of each leader and opened possibilities for negotiation that were blocked at the beginning of the process.

The 'Islands of Agreement' is a manipulative trick that can be applied in various negotiating situations, from family disputes to politics. It can be useful in overcoming deadlocks. The following example demonstrates that borrowing ideas from political negotiation to family negotiation can be very valuable.

A bitter conflict was introduced in one of my Solution-Focused Negotiation classes. A young married couple constantly argued about the appropriate division of the household chores. The clashes created tensions, frustration and an unpleasant atmosphere at home.

The couple seemed to be locked in ongoing frustrating debates and blame games. The wife—*who was seven months pregnant*—complained that her husband almost never helps her with the household chores. She has to do almost all the work by herself. Her husband claimed that his main responsibility is to put food on the table. He is extremely busy at work and does not have the time and energy to do household chores. He claimed that his wife's constant complaints create unnecessary tensions at home.

The wife and her husband agreed to participate in Online Solution-Focused Negotiation in order to resolve their conflict. We used Back-door mediation (two cooperative mediators). A student of mine functioned as the acting mediator and I served as a secret advisor.

The "negotiation" seemed to be desperate positional bargaining. They were in a binary trap (her position versus his). She wanted him to share responsibility for the household chores. He claimed his regular job did not leave any time or energy to help. He is the main financial provider and he felt responsible for the economic welfare of the family that was about to grow (his wife was pregnant). Is it possible to find a negotiable difference in this situation?

A solution of mutual benefit had the potential to improve the quality of their family and personal lives. However, each of them faced a dilemma. On the one hand, the wife and her husband shared the same interests—building and maintaining a happy and peaceful family (cooperative motivation). On the other hand, each of them demanded a different solution to a bitter dispute over the division of the household chores (competitive motivation). To put it differently, both parties faced a classic negotiator's dilemma—ambivalence between cooperative and competitive attitudes.

Effective combination of a mediator-friend (the acting mediator) and a secret advisor (a professional practitioner) helped each of them overcome the negotiator's dilemma. The acting mediator motivated the parties to negotiate good faith solutions to their problem. The secret advisor identified a game changer that enabled them to find an appropriate formula to divide the household chores to the satisfaction of both sides.

The continuation of the negotiation uncovered 'Islands of Agreement'. Both sides agreed that the household chores needed to be done and, in principle, the husband is required to help. This was the first step toward overcoming the binary trap (help or not help). The frustrating debate on the binary question—**Is** the husband required to do household chores in the current circumstances? —was replaced with a constructive negotiation on the non-binary question—**What** conditions require the husband to help by doing some household chores?

Reframing the negotiating question was a turning point. However, the parties still needed another key game changer to identify a negotiable difference. I followed Chris Voss' advice and carefully followed the course of the negotiation.

At a certain point, the husband stated that when he comes home after a long exhausting day at work, he does not have any energy to do household chores. His remark reminded me of the negotiation between Sadat and Begin in the 1978 Camp David Summit. I thought the idea of concluding two agreements might work here also. Indeed, this insight was a resolving game changer.

The key to resolve the conflict was to identify two situations—times when the husband is too tired and times when he is not. The "objective" criterion to distinguish the two situations is the time he returns home from work. Returning home before 7 pm means not too tired, returning after 7 pm means too tired.

Each of the parties prepared two lists. The wife prepared a list of household work that she expected her husband to do when he is tired and a list when he is not tired. The husband also prepared lists of household work he was able and willing to do in each situation. They negotiated the differences in each list (tired and not tired) and concluded two agreements.

On a personal note, I believe there is a golden rule in family relationships: Never argue with your pregnant wife. In this case, I served only as a secret advisor. I helped the couple to identify key game changers in negotiating solutions to an unnecessary conflict.

Problem-Solving Cooperative—Changing Concepts

Solution-Focused Negotiation begins with positional bargaining. Each side is invited to introduce his or her initial position on the issue at stake. They present different and usually opposing demands to solve a joint problem. In their seminal book *Getting to Yes*, Fisher and Ury showed that commitment to positions often leads to a dead-end. It blocks creative thinking and locks the mind in a one-dimensional picture of reality. It is a proven recipe for falling into the binary trap—my position or yours.

Scholars of negotiation have suggested various creative ways to escape a binary trap. Fisher and Ury suggested exploring the interests that motivate parties to adopt firm, rigid and inflexible positions. The psychologist Herbert Kelman recommended analyzing the needs and fears that incentivize negotiators to be entrenched in their positions. The logic of both methods is quite the same.

People have multiple interests and needs that can be satisfied in different ways. The shift in focus—from positions to interests and needs—has the potential to open new possibilities. It can help the parties overcome the binary trap. However, the shift can be challenging—How can we identify the interests, needs and fears of the negotiating parties? How do we describe a problem, which inflamed frustrating positional bargaining, in terms of interests and needs? How do we turn competitive parties—who are deeply involved in positional bargaining—into a problem-solving team committed to find solutions that address the interests, needs and fears of each party?

One method to cope with the transformation problem—turning competitive parties into a problem-solving team—is to introduce new concepts. New concepts can be a key game changer that has the potential to provide different meanings to the negotiation. The issue of trust in negotiation can demonstrate the trick.

'Working Trust' and 'Basic Trust'—Political Dispute

A certain level of trust is needed to successfully conclude Solution-Focused Negotiation. The opposing parties need to be quite certain that they can reach agreements that address their interests, needs and fears. However, in difficult situations of conflict, the required level of trust usually does not exist.

Unfortunately, lack of trust is a central motif in the relationship between opposing parties. Palestinians do not trust Israelis and Israelis do not trust Palestinians. Business partners can lose confidence in each other and become enemies. Husbands and wives can lose faith in the reliability of their spouse. How can one overcome this major obstacle and help the negotiating parties reach an agreement of mutual advantage?

A powerful mediator—such as the President of the United States—is sometimes able to bypass the trust obstacle by compelling opposing parties to reach agreements and providing guarantees for their implementation. Richard Holbrooke, the NATO representative to the Balkans in 1995, succeeded in compelling bitter enemies to reach agreements in former Yugoslavia. He led a three-month brutal peace process that concluded with the Dayton Accords. This Agreement put an end to a bloody civil war that killed about 100,000 people.

Solution-Focused Negotiation is often a voluntary interaction, at least to some degree. Usually, mediators do not have political, economic and military power and leverage. They cannot enforce agreements and they are certainly not able to provide guarantees for their implementation. To cope with the trust problem, it is useful to approach the issue from a different perspective.

Peace and Conflict Studies scholars suggest that we distinguish two kinds of trust—'working trust' and 'basic trust'. 'Working trust'—a term coined by Herbert Kelman—is the belief of each party that the other party is committed to resolve the conflict by peaceful means out of its own selfish interests.[5] 'Basic trust' is a secure confidence in the reliability of the other side.[6]

In difficult situations of conflict—where one party does not believe one word of the other—it is quite impossible to build 'basic trust'. In these sad situations, it is more realistic to focus on building 'working trust' than wasting futile energy in trying to reach the impossible—goal of 'basic trust'. The *Minds of Peace Experiments*—small-scale Israeli-Palestinian Public Negotiating Congresses—demonstrated this issue again and again. My colleagues and I have led these experiments in various forms, formats and locations.[7]

These experiments invite Israeli and Palestinian delegations of ordinary citizens to a Solution-Focused Negotiation. The experiments have two stages: 1. Negotiating trust building measures; and 2. Negotiating a conclusive peace agreement.

The trust building stage is a relationship-building instrument. It is designed to create commitment of the two sides to the process and turn them into a joint problem-solving cooperative. However, an atmosphere of chronic suspicion was in the air at the beginning of each assembly. How do we negotiate trust? How do we build trust in situations of lack of trust? How do we ensure that trust is established?

To cope with this lack-of-trust barrier, the mediators were instructed to encourage the negotiators to follow Adam Smith's famous insight—"It is not from the benevolence of the butcher, the brewer or the baker that we expect our dinner, but from their regard to their own self-interest. We address ourselves not to their humanity but to their self-love, and never talk to them of our own necessities, but of their advantages".[8] The mediators led the negotiators to focus on building 'working trust'. The negotiating parties needed to demonstrate that they believe peace is a social good with mutual benefits. And it is their own self-interest and basic need to reach a peaceful resolution of the conflict.

At the beginning of the negotiation, the mediators asked the parties to present their initial demands for reaching the 'Trust Building Measures' goal. What steps should each side take in order to start building trust? How can each side convince the other that achieving a negotiated peace is in its own best interest? What actions should each party immediately take to demonstrate sincere and genuine commitment to the process?

In most sessions of the Minds of Peace Experiment (MOPE), violence was one of the main concerns of the opposing parties. Both sides demanded commitment to stop all acts of violence. And both parties agreed that violence should be stopped. However, the problem was that violence is a broad concept that means different things to each party. For example, Palestinian prisoners are considered freedom fighters by Palestinians and terrorists by Israelis. The release of prisoners is very important to Palestinians and very difficult for Israelis.

In general, prisoners of a conflict are a major issue in situations of violent intractable conflict. Their society regards them as freedom fighters and heroes who were willing to sacrifice their lives for a just cause. In contrast, the other side (the captor) sees the same prisoners as terrorists or brutal criminals (depending on the type of the conflict). Accordingly, one side sees the release of prisoners as a necessary trust building measure, while the other side sees it as an unacceptable demand that can encourage the use of violence.[9]

Most sessions of the Minds of Peace Experiment began with maximalist demands. Palestinians demanded immediate release of prisoners. Israelis refused this demand out of hand. The two delegations were marching toward a binary trap (release or not release).

To overcome the binary trap, the mediators encouraged the parties to focus on non-binary questions, such as: How can this sensitive issue—the release of Palestinian prisoners—help build trust between the two sides?

This frame—presenting and organizing the problem differently—changed the discussion. It helped the parties replace the frustrating debate—release or not release—with constructive negotiation on the terms for releasing prisoners. Surprisingly, the delegations discovered that this controversial matter can be an incentive that contributes to the progress of the negotiation and the promotion of peace. For example, the released prisoners can become ambassadors of peace.

The agreements of the various MOPE assemblies clearly demonstrate this. Here is an example, taken from an agreement on Trust Building Measures that was reached in one of the assemblies:

Gradual Release of Prisoners:

1. Israel will release Palestinian prisoners in stages according to the progress in the negotiation and security needs.
2. Israel will begin by releasing Palestinian prisoners who did not kill anyone.

Refrain from Violence:

3. Each released prisoner will promise to avoid violent activity.

Ambassadors of Peace:

4. The prisoners will commit to become ambassadors of peace.
5. The prisoners will take an active part in educational programs that explain to the public the importance of reaching peace by peaceful means.

In the negotiation process of the Minds of Peace Experiment, violence is determined by the parties according to their interests, needs and fears. The fate of prisoners is only one issue in the multidimensional discussion on the practical meaning of violence. And violence is only one topic in the effort to build 'working trust' in situations of bloody intractable conflict.

'Working Trust' and 'Basic Trust'—Family Dispute

'Working trust' is a limited form of trust that enables the opposing parties to become a negotiating cooperative. Each side is required to demonstrate its commitment to the process. The 'Trust Building Measures Agreement' in a political dispute needs to address the interests, needs and fears of the opposing parties.

Ironically, in family disputes—when 'basic trust' (a secure confidence in the reliability of the other) exists—lack of trust can still be a barrier to conflict resolution. The negotiators—family members who know each other very well—do not trust the other party to keep and implement commitments. They believe that good intentions are not enough for conflict prevention and resolution.

A well-known trigger of aggressive confrontations is a gap between expectations and reality. This gap creates disappointment, frustration and anger. I remember planning to speak with my wife about an issue that was important to me. I planned a strategy to approach her, I imagined her reactions, and I prepared strong arguments. However, when we met, my wife was in a completely different state of mind. She did not have any energy, patience or willingness to discuss this issue with me. The gap between my desire and passion to discuss the issue and her indifferent attitude was a hot potato. It has the potential to create tension, friction and confrontation.

This was the main problem in one of our case studies. A mediator—who participated in the Negoflict project—invited a mother and her teenage son to participate in an Online Solution-Focused Negotiation. The problem was the son's inappropriate behavior. The son often lost his temper and behaved rudely and aggressively toward his parents and siblings.

Disappointment caused the son to act aggressively. It constantly happened in situations where the child returned home late from school. On the way home, he planned, dreamed and fantasized about using the family's computer. The moment he entered home and saw that the computer is being used by his siblings, he lost his temper.

In the negotiation, it turned out that the son suffers from the consequences of his aggressive behavior. When he calms down, he tends to regret his inappropriate behavior. He promised to make a maximum effort to change his attitude and to peacefully resolve tensions, disputes and conflicts with his siblings. However, his mother did not believe him.

To be more precise, his mother believed the sincere, genuine and honest intentions of her son to change. However, she did not trust his ability to control his impulsive attitude. She reminded him that he has promised several times to modify his behavior but he did not keep his commitments. In critical moments of friction, he continued to lose control.

They needed a different approach to resolve the issue. They needed a game changer. They needed to design a mechanism that could help the child control his attitude and gain his mother's trust. They searched for a mechanism that is not entirely dependent on the child's good will, motivation or ability to control his temper. The mother used her common sense, experience and practical knowledge to suggest ideas that could help solve the problem.

The negotiators (mother and child) agreed on these general rules of conduct in situations of potential clashes:

- One family member will ask for a time-out.
- The conflicting parties will take a break and go to relax in their rooms.
- They will settle the dispute only when they are relaxed and free from distractions.
- In critical moments, they will communicate by signs: one sign for a time-out—"need to relax"—and another sign for a resumption—"ready for peaceful discussion".

Constitutional economists have taught us that 'rules are tools'. It is better to trust general rules of conduct than the good intentions of human beings, especially in times of distress.[10] Rules are designed to help us control our instinctive, automatic and irrational patterns of behavior. Rules enable us to develop constructive habits that can help overcome destructive behavior. In this case, it is better for the child to take a time-out whenever he identifies warning signs of feeling angry (the cue) than to surrender to his automatic and unbeneficial aggressive instinct.

The idea to agree on general rules of conduct was a game changer. It changed the dynamic of the discussion between the negotiators and released the deadlock. The mother—who did not trust the ability of her child to control his temper—was willing to trust his ability to follow a new rule of conduct. The child was happy to gain a new tool in his struggle to control his impulsive nature.

'Working Trust' as a Key Game Changer

'Lack of trust' can be a strategic barrier for entering negotiation. Churchill refused any type of negotiation with Hitler even when the situation seemed to be hopeless. He did not trust Hitler, to say the least. He believed Hitler would deceive any negotiating partner. Any attempt to negotiate with the Führer would be interpreted as a sign of weakness. Churchill was probably right.[11] However, this is an extreme case. In most conflicts we do not confront a Hitler. Most of our adversaries want to stop fighting and end conflicts as much as we do.

Disputing parties who do not trust each other tend to avoid, reject and refuse any negotiating initiative. However, when adversaries meet at the negotiating table, the picture can change. The strategic barrier for initiating negotiation can become a tactical barrier at the negotiation table.

The parties come to negotiate in good faith, accept the rules of the game and commit to the process. But they still do not believe one another. 'Lack of trust' becomes a barrier for successfully concluding the negotiation.

To overcome the 'lack of trust' barrier in Solution-Focused Negotiation, it is recommended to focus on building 'working trust' and relinquishing the aspiration to build 'basic trust'. 'Working trust' is based on two main principles: 1. Negotiators demonstrate that reaching agreements is in their best interest, and 2. Negotiators commit to follow general rules of conduct that enable them to overcome human weaknesses.

The 'working trust' concept coined by Herbert Kelman is a game changer. It enables opposing parties to negotiate and build 'practical trust' in situations of chronic mistrust. The concept is based on the interests, needs and fears of the negotiating parties and not on their good intensions and altruistic motivations. This negotiating construction ('working trust') is one of the building blocks in the effort to turn opposing parties into a negotiating cooperative and successfully conclude Solution-Focused Negotiation.

Consensus-Building—Supportive Environment

Disputing parties are often locked in their positions and do not constructively listen to one another. They are caught in a binary trap (my position or yours). They are deeply involved in a destructive blame game.

Even a skilled mediator may not find 'Islands of Agreement' and cannot identify negotiable differences. Attempts to present the conflicting problem in terms of interests and needs may also not work. It may be necessary to ask for help and involve additional players in the effort to resolve the conflict.

The consensus-building process is designed to involve—directly and indirectly—key players in the negotiating process. The idea is to create pro-negotiating coalitions that can create a supportive environment for the negotiation process. Key players can have a valuable impact on the opposing parties and the negotiating process. They can help, create and identify the desired key game changers. Let me demonstrate.

A student in my class described a bitter conflict with her younger brother. At first glance the situation seemed hopeless. The fight was about the big bedroom in their home. The sister (my student) insisted on following the family tradition—the oldest sister gets the big bedroom. The bedroom became available when the oldest sister married and left home. My student thought it was only natural that she should have the big bedroom.

Her younger brother objected and rejected this idea. He claimed the big bedroom for himself. He presented three justifications: (1) The tradition applies only to sisters (females) and he is a male; (2) The room he has is not large enough to contain his belongings; and (3) He has a girlfriend and they need privacy in a larger room.

We did a simulation in class to develop a strategy that could help my student (the sister) cope with the conflict. She warned us that her brother is stubborn and will never give up his desire to have the big bedroom. Another student of mine invited the siblings to participate in Online Solution-Focused Negotiation under her guidance and mediation.

The mediator-student opened the negotiation by introducing the problem. She asked the parties to present their initial positions. As we anticipated, the picture was quite gloomy. The parties were locked in a binary zero-sum game. They were entrenched in painful and hopeless positional bargaining. Each one claimed the big room and showed no intention to give up. It looked impossible to find a negotiable difference and analyzing the conflict in terms of interests, needs and fears was no help.

The mediator asked for a one-day time-out. She reminded the siblings that they have the responsibility to maintain a peaceful atmosphere at home. She emphasized that it is possible to divorce a spouse, but impossible to divorce a sibling.[12] She instructed them to make a maximum effort to come up with creative solutions to their problem.

In the second session (after the time-out), the mediator surprised the siblings. She made a dramatic move that changed the zero-sum game. She told them that she contacted their mother and asked for her advice. Their mother suggested enlarging "the pie" by adding two attractive issues to the negotiating table—the laundry room and a new closet. She proposed that the sister receive the laundry room—which can be turned into a study room—and a new closet if the sister will agree to remain in her bedroom.

The siblings accepted the mother's proposal and the conflict was resolved. In the agreement they added the commitment of the brother to renegotiate the arrangement in good faith if their circumstances change. For example, if the sister gets a serious boyfriend and needs the big bedroom.

It is quite common for disputing parties to believe they are fighting over a fixed object. They see a one-dimensional picture of the very essence of the conflict that cannot be changed. They believe that the conflict is about a well-defined resource. Countries fight over a well-defined territory;

divorcing couples struggle to find the appropriate division of their property; and siblings try to maximize their share of an inheritance.

It is a well-known mistake to believe that the essence of the conflict is a fixed resource. Scholars of negotiation have taught us that the object of a conflict is almost never fixed. It can shrink, get larger and even become multidimensional. It is all a matter of perspective. State leaders, who fight over the same territory, can be a useful example.

The leaders see the disputed territory as a fixed goal. However, the territory is not fixed. It can be diminished significantly. For example, a war can destroy the land and decrease its value. And, the territory can also be enlarged. For example, the conflict is not only about the land. It is also about the stability of the region and the safety and well-being of its citizens.

Giving the 'object of the conflict' ("the pie") different meanings, sizes and dimensions can be a game changer. However, it can be a challenge to find the most effective and useful way to do it. The conflicting parties can be entrenched in their positions. The vision, information and knowledge of the mediator can be also limited. Involving pro-negotiation elements in the conflict resolution effort can help the parties examine the conflict and its implications from different perspectives and can be a useful method to overcome barriers.

Consensus-building scholars look at negotiation as a process of building supportive coalitions. Involving pro-negotiation elements in the effort to resolve the conflict by peaceful means can make a valuable contribution to the process. It can help the conflicting parties examine the situation from different—imagined or unimagined—perspectives. This can be the way to find key game changers that help overcome a deadlock. The consensus-building process can be applied in various types of negotiations—from two-party to multiparty talks—in almost all walks of life, from family disputes to politics.

Consensus-building scholars replace the "What is the optimal solution to the conflict?" question with "Who should be involved in the effort to reach a sustainable negotiated solution to the conflict and how?" According to this perspective, coalition-building—involving various players in the effort to resolve a conflict—is needed to begin, support, conclude and implement effective negotiated agreements.

Concluding Remarks

This chapter suggests looking at Solution-Focused Negotiation as a discovery procedure. It is the art of detecting, creating or constructing key game changers. In the most difficult cases of conflict, key game changers are required to initiate a negotiating process, maintain it and conclude agreements of mutual advantage.

The main focus here is on key game changers that enable negotiating partners to successfully conclude the negotiation process and resolve their conflict by peaceful means. The assumptions are: disputing parties are engaged in Solution-Focused Negotiation, they are motivated to resolve their conflict by peaceful means, and they are committed to the rules, framework and structure of the interaction. However, they do not know how to proceed in the negotiating process, settle their differences and resolve the conflict.

The parties need key game changers to progress and successfully conclude negotiations. The challenge is to find a systematic methodology that helps mediators identify key game changers during a negotiation. This chapter describes the first steps for doing this.

Negotiation is a broad concept that has different meanings to different people. There are different types of negotiating processes that suggest different methods and procedures to cope with conflicts. Different types of negotiation require different types of key game changers.

The main focus here is on three categories of negotiation—bargaining, problem-solving and consensus-building. Each category offers different methods to discover key game changers. I demonstrated the relationship between each of these processes and a relevant key game changer.

Bargaining is the most intuitive negotiation process. It is a competitive confrontation between the demands of conflicting parties. In the most difficult cases, each side sees only two options: "mine" or "yours". They are trapped in a binary debate. *'Islands of Agreement'*—points of agreement within disagreements—can be a key game changer. They can lead the parties to identify negotiable differences that enable them to escape the binary trap.

Problem-Solving is a cooperative mode of negotiation. The interaction focuses on the interests, needs and fears of the parties instead of their positions. This shift opens possibilities for cooperation. It rests on the assumption that people have different interests and needs that can be satisfied in different ways. *Changing Concepts*—presenting central issues, such as trust, in terms of interests and needs—can be a key game changer. It transforms hopeless positional debate into a constructive problem-solving interaction. It helps the parties look at conflicting issues as shared problems that they need to solve together. I showed that the concept 'working trust'—trust that is based on interests rather than good will—opens possibilities for cooperation in desperate situations of chronic distrust. It enables conflicting parties to be converted into a problem-solving team and conclude agreements.

Consensus-Building is a process of building supportive coalitions. Consensus-building practitioners focus on the question—"Who should be involved in the effort to resolve the conflict and how?" The idea is to involve—directly or indirectly—*key players* in the effort to reach negotiated agreements of mutual benefit. Key players can approach the situation from a different perspective, illuminate the difficulties in a different light and open new possibilities for discussion. They can help the parties escape a deadlock.

Table 7.1 summarizes the correlations between the three negotiating processes and relevant game changers.

Discovering key game changers during a negotiating interaction can be a masterpiece. The table below presents only the correlation between three types of negotiation and relevant key game changers. The actual requirement is to provide a map of valuable insights (game changers) that can help mediators and negotiators overcome negotiation deadlocks.

The next book suggests that we approach the use of game changers from a different perspective. It proposes a model to classify classic barriers to conflict resolution. This model enables us to create a database of insights that can overcome various barriers. This database of correlations between classic barriers and insights can be part of a computerized recommendation system for Solution-Focused Negotiation.

Table 7.1 Correlations between negotiating processes and key game changers

Negotiation type	Negotiating process	Key game changers	Results
Bargaining	Competition	Identifying 'Islands of Agreement'	Discovering negotiable differences
Problem-solving	Cooperation	Introducing central concepts in terms of interests and needs	Addressing the main concerns of the parties on a basis of reciprocity
Consensus-building	Coalition-building	Involving key players in a negotiating effort	Approaching the conflict from different perspectives

A computerized recommendation system, which provides valuable insights according to the logic of the situation, can improve the performances of human mediators.

Notes

1. See Hayek (1945).
2. See Fisher et al. (2011).
3. Ibid.
4. Voss was a hostage negotiator. His original problem is to "win" the negotiation. His negotiating efforts and skills are designed to release hostages at minimum risk and cost. However, his book points out that splitting the difference is not the optimal result for opposing sides in different kinds of negotiation in various dimensions of our social life. See Voss (2016).
5. See Kelman (2005).
6. See Giddens (1990).
7. http://mindsofpeace.org/.
8. See Smith (1776).
9. See Mitchell (1999).
10. See, for example, Hayek (1967).
11. See Mnookin (2010).
12. The original saying is: "You can divorce your spouse, but you cannot divorce your children".

References

Fisher, Roger, Ury, William L. & Patton, Bruce. 2011. *Getting to Yes: Negotiating agreement without giving in.* New York: Penguin Books.

Giddens, Anthony. 1990. *The Consequences of Modernity.* Cambridge: Polity Press.

Hayek, Friedrich August. 1945. The Use of Knowledge in Society. *American Economic Review* xxxv (4): 519-530.

Hayek, Friedrich August. 1967. *Studies in Philosophy, Politics and Economics.* Chicago: University of Chicago Press.

Kelman, Herbert C. 2005. Building trust among enemies: The central challenge for international conflict resolution. *International Journal of Intercultural Relations*, 29 (6): 639-650.

Mitchell, George John. 1999. *Making Peace.* New York, NY: Alfred A. Knopf.

Mnookin, Robert H. 2010. *Bargaining with the devil: When to negotiate, when to fight*. New York, Toronto and Sydney: Simon and Schuster.

Smith, Adam. 1981. *An Inquiry into the Nature and Causes of the Wealth of Nations*. Indianapolis: Liberty Classic.

Voss, Christopher & Raz, Tahl. 2016. *Never Split the Difference: Negotiating as if your life depended on it*. London, UK: Random House Business.

In Conclusion

Solution-Focused Negotiation is a powerful instrument to cope with conflicts. It engages disputing parties in intensive efforts to reach practical and enforceable solutions to their struggles. The initiative can be applied in almost all dimensions of our social life, from family disputes to politics.

Solution-Focused Negotiation rests on three pillars: ***Transformation***—turning opposing parties into a negotiating cooperative; ***Practicality***—focusing the talks on practical solutions to a negotiable problem; and ***Discovery***—detecting key game changers.

I have been engaged—directly and indirectly—in dozens of Solution-Focused Negotiations. I have frequently been asked about the permanence of successful interactions—"Do you think the conflict has really been resolved?"; "Do you believe the parties will finally stop fighting?"; "Do you think the negotiated agreements are sustainable?".

One of the first examples in this book is the Atlantic City Conference of 1929. Leaders of crime families came to negotiate principles for cooperation. They were engaged in Solution-Focused Negotiation. The outcomes of the summit were a big success from the criminal's point of view. It changed the operations of the crime families in the US.

Historians of crime believe the Atlantic City Conference laid the foundations for the establishment of a National Crime Syndicate in America. It led to a change in the social identity of criminals. Gangsters in rival gangs began to see themselves as partners in the national syndicate, at least to some extent.

The National Crime Syndicate became the umbrella organization for the crime families. It influenced the identity, attitude and actions of gangsters. Criminals developed a national identity—"I'm part of the American National

Crime Syndicate"—in addition to their regional identity—"I'm a member of the local crime family". Negotiations that involve a change in identity can have sustainable results.

The psychologist Herbert Kelman, who focused on international conflicts, distinguished three types of peace products—settlements, conflict resolutions and reconciliations. Settlements are the outcome of successful interest-based negotiations. Conflict resolutions are the outcome of successful attempts to reach agreements that address the needs and fears of conflicting parties. Reconciliations are the outcome of peace processes that involve a change in the identity of rival parties.[1]

Kelman believed processes that involve an "I" becomes "We" change in the identity of the parties have the greatest potential to bring sustainable results. Kelman's observation helps to understand the long-lasting success of certain peacemaking initiatives, such as the Atlantic City Conference of 1929. However, the focus of this book is elsewhere.

Social life is dynamic. It brings ongoing challenges to our daily experience. People often find themselves involved in tensions, frictions and conflicts. They compete, cooperate, fight and reconcile. The question is—How do we bring the culture of conflict resolution to our daily life?

Solution-Focused Negotiation is a deal-making and relationship-building instrument. It can be applied in almost all dimensions of our social life—from family disputes to politics. My students, my colleagues and I have demonstrated that online communication can facilitate the use of this powerful social tool. Computer technology can bring the art of Solution-Focused Negotiation to almost all of us. It can pave the way for people to make constructive negotiation and mediation keystone habits. This is the goal of the Negoflict project that my colleagues and I are working on.

The Negoflict project focuses on building a digital platform for Solution-Focused Negotiation. The project is designed to improve the capability of people to handle tensions, frictions and confrontations in their lives.

Notes

1. See Kelman (2010).

References

Kelman, Herbert C. 2010. Conflict resolution and reconciliation: A social-psychological perspective on ending violent conflict between identity groups. *Landscapes of Violence*, 1 (1): Article 5.

Uncited References

Allan, Kenneth. 2007. *The Social Lens: An Invitation to Social and Sociological Theory*. Thousand Oaks, London and New Delhi: Sage Publications.

Aubert, Vilhelm. 1963. Competition and dissensus: two types of conflict and of conflict resolution. *Journal of Conflict Resolution*, 7 (1): 26-42.

Axelrod, Robert M. 1984. *The Evolution of Cooperation*. New York: Basic Books.

Azar, Edward E., Paul Jureidini, and Ronald McLaurin. 1978. Protracted Social Conflict; Theory and Practice in the Middle East. *Journal of Palestine Studies*, 8 (1): 41-60.

Banks, Michael. 1984. The evolution of international relations theory, in Michael Banks (Ed.), *Conflict in world society: A new perspective on international relations*. Sussex, UK: Wheatsheaf Books.

Bar-Siman-Tov, Yaacov. 2007. Dialectic Between Conflict Management and Conflict Resolution, in Yaacov Bar-Siman-Tov (Ed.), *The Israeli-Palestinian Conflict: From Conflict Resolution to Conflict Management*. New York: Palgrave Macmillan.

Beardsley, Kyle. 2011. *The Mediation Dilemma*. Ithaca: Cornell University Press.

Benjamin, Robert D. 1995. The mediator as trickster: The folkloric figure as professional role model. *Conflict Resolution Quarterly*, 13 (2): 131-149.

References

Critchley, David. 2009. *The Origin of Organized Crime in America: The New York City Mafia, 1891–1931.* London: Routledge/

Friedman, Gary & Himmelstein, Jack. 2008. *Challenging conflict: Mediation through understanding.* Chicago: American Bar Association.

Galtung, Johan. 1976. *Peace, War and Defense: Essays in Peace Research, vol. 2.* Copenhagen: Christian Ejlers Forlag,

Handelman, Sapir & Chowdhury, Jyoti. 2017. The Limits of Political-Elite Diplomacy: Leaders, People and Social Conflicts. *Israel Affairs*, 23 (3): 468-495

Handelman, Sapir and Pearson, Frederic S. 2014. Peacemaking in Intractable Conflict: A Contractualist Approach. *International Negotiation*, 19 (1): 1-34

Handelman, S. 2009. *Thought Manipulation: The Use and Abuse of Psychological Trickery: The Use and Abuse of Psychological Trickery.* Santa Barbara, California: ABC-CLIO.

Handelman, Sapir. 2011. The Bangladesh approach to the Palestinian-Israeli struggle: A desperate strategy to cope with a state of emergency. *International Journal of Conflict Management*, 22(1): 75-88.

Handelman, Sapir. 2012a. The Minds of Peace Experiment: A Laboratory for People-to-People Diplomacy. *Israel Affairs*, 18 (1): 1-153.

Hirst, David & Beeson, Irene. 1981. *Sadat.* London: Faber and Faber.

Hoffman, David A. 2011. Mediation and the art of shuttle diplomacy. *Negotiation Journal*, 27 (3): 263-309.

Hopmann, P. Terrence. 1995. Two Paradigms of Negotiation: Bargaining and Problem Solving. *The ANNALS of the American Academy of Political and Social Science*, 542 (1): 24-47.

International Commission of Jurists. 1972. *The Events in East Pakistan, 1971. A legal study by the Secretariat of the International Commission of Jurists.* Geneva https://icj2.wpenginepowered.com/wp-content/uploads/1972/06/Bangladesh-events-East-Pakistan-1971-thematic-report-1972-eng.pdf

Kelman, Herbert C. 1985. Overcoming the Psychological Barrier: An Analysis of the Egyptian-Israeli Peace Process. *Negotiation Journal*, 1 (3): 213-234.

Kelman, Herbert C. 1997. Some determinants of the Oslo breakthrough. *International Negotiation*, 2 (2): 183-194.

Kelman, Herbert C. 2005a. The Psychological Impact of the Sadat Visit on Israeli Society. *Peace and Conflict: Journal of Peace Psychology*, 11 (2): 111-136.

Kelman, Herbert C. 2007. The Israeli–Palestinian Peace Process and Its Vicissitudes: Insights from Attitude Theory. *American Psychologist*, 63 (4): 287-303.

Mnookin, Robert H. 1992. Why negotiations fail: An exploration of barriers to the resolution of conflict. *The Ohio State Journal on Dispute Resolution*, 8 (2): 235-249.

Popper, Karl Raimund. 1959. *The Logic of Scientific Discovery.* New York, NY: Basic Books.

Popper, Karl Raimund. 1994. Models, Instruments and Truth, in Mark Amadeus Notturno (Ed.), *The Myth of the Framework: In Defense of Science and Rationality.* London & New York: Routledge.

Putnam, Robert D. 1988. Diplomacy and Domestic Politics: The Logic of Two-Level Games. *International Organization*, 42 (3): 427-460.

Quandt, William B. 2015. *Camp David: peacemaking and politics*. Washington: Brookings Institution Press.

Ross, Lee & Stillinger, Constance. 1991. Barriers to Conflict Resolution. *Negotiation Journal*, 7 (4): 389-404.

Schmidt, Eric, Rosenberg, Jonathan, Eagle & Alan. 2019. *Trillion Dollar Coach: The Leadership Playbook of Silicon Valley's Bill Campbell*. New York: HarperCollins.

Sifakis, Carl. 2001. *The Encyclopedia of American Crime, 2nd ed.*, New York: Facts on File.

Smith, Adam. 1981. *An Inquiry into the Nature and Causes of the Wealth of Nations*. Indianapolis: Liberty Classic.

Sparks, Allister Haddon. 1994. *Tomorrow Is Another Country: The Inside Story of South Africa's Negotiated Revolution*. Sandton, Sout1h Africa: Struik Book Distributors.

Szasz, Thomas S. (1974). *The myth of mental illness: Foundations of a theory of personal conduct*. New York: Harper & Row Publishers.

Thompson, Leonard. 2014. *A history of South Africa*, Third Edition. New Haven and London: Yale University Press.

Touval, Saadia & Zartman, I. William.1985. *International Mediation in Theory and Practice*. Boulder, CO: Westview Press.

Vuković, Siniša. 2011. Strategies and Bias in International Mediation. *Cooperation and Conflict*, 46 (1): 113-119.

Waltz, Kenneth N. 1979. *Theory of International Politics*. Reading, MA: Addison-Wesley.

Zartman, I. William. 2009. Interest, Leverage and Public Opinion in Mediation. *International Negotiation* 14 (1): 1-5.

Putnam, Robert D. 1988. Diplomacy and Domestic Politics: The Logic of Two-Level Games. *International Organization*, 42 (3): 427-460.

Quandt, William B. 2015. *Camp David: peacemaking and politics*. Washington: Brookings Institution Press.

Ross, Lee & Stillinger, Constance. 1991. Barriers to Conflict Resolution. *Negotiation Journal*, 7 (4): 389-404.

Schmidt, Eric, Rosenberg, Jonathan, Eagle & Alan. 2019. *Trillion Dollar Coach: The Leadership Playbook of Silicon Valley's Bill Campbell*. New York: HarperCollins.

Sifakis, Carl. 2001. *The Encyclopedia of American Crime, 2nd ed.*, New York: Facts on File.

Smith, Adam. 1981. *An Inquiry into the Nature and Causes of the Wealth of Nations*. Indianapolis: Liberty Classic.

Sparks, Allister Haddon. 1994. *Tomorrow Is Another Country: The Inside Story of South Africa's Negotiated Revolution*. Sandton, Sout1h Africa: Struik Book Distributors.

Szasz, Thomas S. (1974). *The myth of mental illness: Foundations of a theory of personal conduct*. New York: Harper & Row Publishers.

Thompson, Leonard. 2014. *A history of South Africa*, Third Edition. New Haven and London: Yale University Press.

Touval, Saadia & Zartman, I. William.1985. *International Mediation in Theory and Practice*. Boulder, CO: Westview Press.

Vuković, Siniša. 2011. Strategies and Bias in International Mediation. *Cooperation and Conflict*, 46 (1): 113-119.

Waltz, Kenneth N. 1979. *Theory of International Politics*. Reading, MA: Addison-Wesley.

Zartman, I. William. 2009. Interest, Leverage and Public Opinion in Mediation. *International Negotiation* 14 (1): 1-5.

Index

A
Academia 53
Agassi, Joseph 85
Al-Aqsa Mosque 57
All-Party Talks 63–67
anchor 91
antisemitism 22
Appeasement 48
Arab-Israeli conflict 5, 21–24, 38, 40
Arafat, Yasser 6
Atlantic City Conference (1929) 5, 75, 143, 144
Austria 46
Awami League 106, 107

B
Bangladesh 108
Barak, Ehud 5
bargaining 19, 25, 30, 33, 45, 49–52, 58, 62, 68–70, 83, 105, 113, 115, 118, 121–127, 129, 136, 138, 139
Barriers
    strategic 2, 21, 22, 26–31, 36, 37, 40–42, 105, 106, 114, 118, 134, 135
    tactical 2, 21, 22, 26, 28, 36, 40–42, 135
BATNA (Best Alternative to a Negotiated Agreement) 107
Begin, Menachem 5, 14, 21, 23, 25, 26, 29–34, 36–41, 118–120, 125, 126, 128
Bengal 106
Bhutto, Zulfikar Ali 107, 108
binary game 103, 104, 107, 108
binary problem 99–103, 105, 112–115
binary question 64, 100, 101, 111–113, 128
binary trap 99, 103–106, 108–111, 113, 114, 126–129, 131, 135, 138
blame game 9, 15, 16, 27, 88, 91, 127, 135
Blum, Gabriella 34, 125
Bosnia 51, 52

Index

Brief Solution-Focused Therapy 17, 91, 114, 119
Buchanan, James 52, 71, 97
Burton, John 54–56, 58, 61

C

Camp David 5, 6, 11, 14, 15, 21, 25, 29–32, 34, 36–41, 69, 113, 120, 125, 128
Carter, Jimmy 5, 14, 21, 22, 24–26, 29–33, 38–41
Chamberlain, Neville 46–48
Christianity 11, 15, 57
Churchill, Winston 48, 95, 134
civil war 52, 54, 83, 108, 130
clash of civilizations 11
Clinton, Bill 5, 16
coalitions 23, 38, 49, 65, 68, 69, 77, 83, 105, 124, 135, 137, 139
Coban Missile Crisis 12, 51
cognitive bias 107–110
Cold War 22, 51, 108
commitment 14, 15, 17–19, 25, 28, 64, 65, 76, 83, 90, 94, 96, 117, 129–133, 136
competition
 constructive 52, 83
 destructive 52, 53, 68, 70, 83, 121
Conflict Analysis and Resolution 43, 54, 122
conflict of interests 7, 28
conflict management 6, 43
conflict resolution 2, 5, 6, 12, 13, 19, 21, 23, 24, 27, 29, 33, 38, 39, 43, 55, 58, 78, 79, 89, 91, 94, 99, 102, 105, 106, 108, 112–114, 121, 124, 133, 137, 139, 144
consensus-building 19, 30, 49, 50, 59, 62–65, 68–70, 77, 83, 121, 123, 124, 135, 137–139
Constitution 75, 76, 83, 106, 107
Constitutional Economics 52, 83, 134
Contractualism 40, 49, 50, 59, 61, 62
Control Communication 55, 58
Cooperation 5, 7, 8, 29, 32, 54, 62, 68, 80, 83, 138, 139, 143
Corona crisis 28
creating value 80–83
Cuba 51
Cuban Missile Crisis 12, 51
Czechoslovakia 46–48

D

Dayton Accords 52, 130
deadlock 19, 27, 36, 108, 115, 119, 120, 124, 127, 134, 137, 139
dealbreaker 105, 107, 115
debate
 binary 111, 115, 122, 138
 historical 16, 49, 50, 84–90
de Klerk Willem 108
deterrence 50–52, 54
devil 45, 46, 48, 49, 63, 64, 75
difference
 negotiable 34, 112, 122, 125–128, 135, 136, 138, 139
diplomacy
 closed-door 29
 people-to-people 38
 political-elite 38, 61, 62
 public 38, 39, 62, 65
divorce 6, 7, 15–17, 19, 32, 35, 41, 42, 59, 66, 69, 81, 99–101, 112, 125, 136, 140
Dublin 16, 66

E

Ego 53
Egypt 5, 14, 22, 23, 25, 30, 32–34, 36–42, 69, 113, 118–120, 126
Einstein, Albert 18

emotional mind 2, 87, 110
emotional weaknesses 2
empathy
　tactical 85, 86, 115
Europe 46, 47

Falsification Principle 10
Fisher, Roger 2, 72, 84, 94, 102, 103, 105, 113–115, 125, 129, 140
Fisher, Ronald 58, 71
Freud, Sigmund 109

game changer
　initiating 117, 118
　motivating 117
　resolving 118–120, 126–128
Gaza 31, 37
Geneva initiative 89
Germany 46–49
Getting to Yes (Fisher, Ury and Patton) 2, 84, 94, 102, 105, 125, 129
Gilboa, Eytan 29, 43
Good Friday Agreement 35, 60, 61, 68, 78

habits 13, 55, 76, 85, 103, 104, 106, 115, 134, 144
Hayek, Friedrich 85, 97, 140
history trap, see also historical debate 16
Hitler, Adolf 46–49, 134
Holbrooke, Richard 51, 130
Holocaust 22
household chores 12, 86, 92, 115, 127, 128,
Huntington, Samuel 11, 71, 76, 97

ideal mediator 77, 120, 121
India 106, 107
inheritance 81, 82, 92, 125, 137
interests-based negotiation 105, 118
International Relations 30, 39, 50, 53, 54, 61
Intractable conflict 21, 22, 24, 39, 42, 52, 54, 58, 59, 61, 66, 80, 83, 88, 91, 101, 131, 132
IRA (Irish Republican Army) 63, 79
Irish Republic 59, 60, 64, 65, 67
irrational mind, see also emotional mind 46, 84, 85, 109
irresolvable conflict 6, 8
Islam 11, 15, 57
Islands of agreement 33, 34, 36, 125–128, 135, 138, 139
Israel 1, 5, 14, 22, 23, 25, 27, 30–34, 36–42, 56, 57, 69, 87, 88, 99, 100, 113, 118–120, 126, 132
Israeli-Palestinian conflict 6, 11, 12, 39, 42, 52, 58, 101

Jerusalem
　holy places 10, 11, 83
Jordan 23, 37
Judaism 11, 15, 57
Judgment of Solomon 122
Justice
　historical 89, 90
　practical 89, 90

Kahneman, Daniel 45, 84, 109, 110, 115
Kant, Immanuel 75
Kelman, Herbert 36, 84, 89, 129, 130, 135, 144
Kennedy, John 51

Kennedy, Robert 51
Khan, Yahya 107
Khrushchev, Nikita 51

L

London 16, 55, 56, 58, 66
London Workshop 56, 58

M

Machiavellian Prince 120
Malhotra, Deepak 41
Mallon, Seamus 35
Mandela, Nelson 108
manipulation 50, 55, 62
mediation
    back-door 80, 81, 83, 92, 93, 103, 127
Meir, Golda 14
Middle East 5, 14, 17, 22, 25, 30, 34, 36–40, 58, 118, 119, 126
Minds of Peace Experiment 12, 56, 89, 130–132
miracle question 17
mirror image 16
Mitchell, George
    Principles 64
Mnookin, Robert 45
Munich Agreement 47, 48
Mussolini, Benito 47

N

narrative
    constructed 88
National Crime Syndicate 76, 143
Negoflict 3, 85, 93, 133, 144
negotiable conflict, *see also* resaleable conflict 115
negotiable problem 10, 13, 15, 18, 19, 105, 115, 117, 143
negotiated agreement 21, 26, 60, 62, 81, 97, 104, 105, 107, 111, 112, 114, 137, 139, 143

negotiated solution 6, 10, 12, 24, 28, 79, 82, 105, 121, 137
negotiating cooperative 13–15, 76–78, 82, 90, 96, 117, 132, 135, 143
negotiator's dilemma 7, 8, 32, 127, 128
Netanyahu, Benjamin 82, 99, 105, 106
Never Split the Difference (Voss) 2, 85, 125
non-binary problem 99, 100, 102, 104, 105
non-binary question 64, 100, 101, 111, 113, 114, 128, 131
non-negotiable conflict, *see also* irresolvable conflict 115
non-negotiable problem 10, 15, 17, 102, 105
Northern Ireland 16, 17, 35, 49, 58–60, 61, 63–65, 67, 68, 78–80, 87, 108
nuclear war 50, 51

O

October war of 1973 14
online Solution-Focused Negotiation 9, 13, 56, 81, 86, 92, 93, 103, 111, 127, 133, 136
optimism 80, 125
organized crime 5, 75
Oslo accords 37

P

Pakistan
    East 106–108
    West 106, 107
Pakistan People's Party (PPP) 106
Parkinson Northcote 65
paradox of stalemate 79
peace 5, 11, 12, 14, 16, 17, 21, 22, 23, 24, 25, 26, 29–43, 47–54,

56–58, 60–68, 78–80, 82, 83, 89, 100–103, 108, 113, 118–120, 125, 126, 130–132, 144
Peace and Conflict Studies 40, 53, 61, 62, 83, 130
Peacebuilding 42, 43, 50, 102
Peacekeeping 42, 43, 50, 102, 118
Peacemaking 6, 24, 32, 38, 39, 43, 50, 54–56, 58, 60–65, 78, 80, 102, 108, 114, 118, 127, 144
pie 19, 136, 137
Pluralism 40, 49, 50, 53, 58, 61, 62
point of no return 26, 30, 31, 32
Popper, Karl 10, 85, 117
positional bargaining 25, 69, 105, 113, 115, 118, 123, 125, 127, 129, 136
power mediator 30–32, 40, 120
practical knowledge 81, 120, 134
pragmatic question 10, 15, 16
problem-solving 10, 19, 29, 30, 31, 42, 43, 47, 49, 50, 53, 55–58, 61, 62, 68–70, 77, 83, 84, 88, 90, 100, 117, 118, 120–124, 129, 130, 138, 139
provocation 26, 57, 85, 93
public negotiating assembly 57
public opinion 57, 62, 63
Pyrrhic victory 8

Rahman, Mujibur 107
rational mind 2, 46, 84–87, 109
Realism 30, 39, 40, 49, 50, 52–54, 58, 61, 62
reciprocity 36, 51, 54, 68, 90, 104, 114, 119, 123, 126, 139
recommendation system 139, 140
reconciliation 144
resolvable conflict 2, 6, 8, 10, 102
revolution 3, 18, 38, 58, 64, 78, 80, 105, 108

ripe moment 78, 79
Robert, Henry Martyn 47, 65
Robert's Rules of Order 47
Rules 2, 5, 9, 10, 13–15, 17, 19, 20, 47, 48, 52, 65, 75–77, 83–86, 90, 92, 94, 96, 103, 134, 135, 138

Sadat, Anwar 5, 14, 21, 23, 118, 119, 125
save face 28
Schelling, Thomas 50
Sinai Peninsula 23, 32, 36, 69, 72, 113, 118, 120
Six Day War 23
Sharon, Ariel 57
shuttle negotiation 31, 40, 41, 90, 91
Smith, Adam 130, 140
social sciences 49
South Africa
  Apartheid 22, 78–80
Soviet Union 51
Sunk-cost fallacy 109, 110
Sunningdale 35, 60, 61, 63
super mediator 42, 77, 81, 92, 95, 96
support system 42, 91, 92, 96

talks about talks 65
Tel-Aviv 1, 23, 56
Temple Mount 57
Troubles (conflict in Northern Ireland) 59, 60
Trust
  basic 129, 130, 132, 133, 135
  building measures 57, 130–132
  practical 135
  working 129–132, 134, 135, 139

turning point 5, 21, 23, 24, 60, 93, 111, 115, 118, 121, 124, 128
Turkey 51
Tversky and Kahneman 91, 108–110
Two State Solution 38, 42, 101

U

United Kingdom 46, 48, 59, 60
Ury, William 2, 50, 84, 94, 102, 103, 105, 113–115, 125, 129
United States 130

V

visionary mediator, *see also* super mediator 14, 77, 94–96

Voss, Chris 2, 85, 86, 121, 125, 128, 140

W

West Bank 31, 37, 38
World Society Paradigm 54
World War II 12, 95

Y

Yugoslavia 51, 130

Z

Zartman, William 79, 80, 97
zero-sum game 19, 105, 107, 125, 126, 136

GPSR Compliance

The European Union's (EU) General Product Safety Regulation (GPSR) is a set of rules that requires consumer products to be safe and our obligations to ensure this.

If you have any concerns about our products, you can contact us on

ProductSafety@springernature.com

In case Publisher is established outside the EU, the EU authorized representative is:

Springer Nature Customer Service Center GmbH
Europaplatz 3
69115 Heidelberg, Germany

www.ingramcontent.com/pod-product-compliance
Lightning Source LLC
LaVergne TN
LVHW011008250326
834688LV00004B/137